W9-AYB-675

Shaw: Seven Critical Essays

Seven papers presented at the

Shaw Seminars, Niagara-on-the-Lake

1966-1968

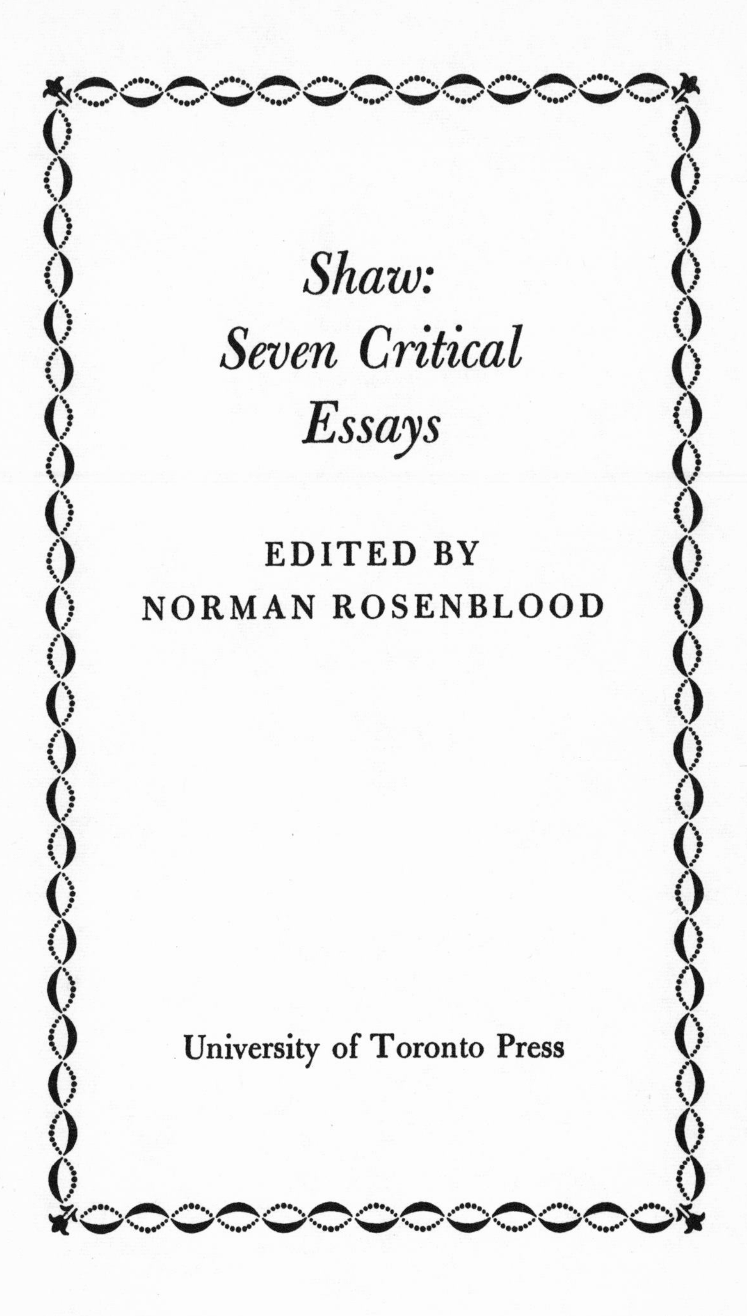

Shaw: Seven Critical Essays

EDITED BY
NORMAN ROSENBLOOD

University of Toronto Press

University of Toronto Press

Toronto and Buffalo

reprinted 1972

printed in Canada

ISBN 0-8020-1731-2

ISBN microfiche 0-8020-0003-7

LC 75-151388

Contributors

NORMAN ROSENBLOOD
Assistant Professor of English, McMaster University

ALAN DOWNER
Professor of English, Princeton University

STANLEY WEINTRAUB
Editor of The Shaw Review
Professor of English, Pennsylvania State University

R. B. PARKER
Professor of English, Trinity College, University of Toronto
Director of the Graduate Centre for the Study of Drama, Massey College, University of Toronto

WARREN SYLVESTER SMITH
Professor of Theatre Arts, Director of General Education in the Arts, Pennsylvania State University

JAMES D. MERRITT
Assistant Professor of English, Brooklyn College of the City University of New York

CLIFFORD LEECH
Professor of English, University of Toronto

MARTIN MEISEL
Professor of English, Columbia University

Contents

Acknowledgments

I should like to thank Dr. Togo Salmon of McMaster University for his encouragement and support.

This book has been published with the help of a grant from the Humanities Research Council of Canada, using funds provided by the Canada Council.

N.R.

Introduction

The essays in this collection were read at the Shaw Seminars held at Brock University, St. Catharines, Ontario, and at the Shaw Festival, Niagara-on-the-Lake, during the summers of 1966, 1967, and 1968. Like its colleague seminar at Stratford, the Shaw Seminar is designed to enhance the playgoer's understanding and appreciation of live drama by bringing together people with broad ranges of interests in the theatre. These essays represent the current thriving interest in both live theatre and engaging criticism.

Essays of this kind confront an editor with two problems. The first is Shaw's view of the critic. One remembers with pleasure and pain his concise description of the drama critic: "I think very few people know how troublesome dramatic critics are. It is not that they are morally worse than other people; but they know nothing. Or, rather, it is a good deal worse than that: they know everything wrong." Shaw's judgment might be construed as either a characteristic exaggeration or a challenge. If a challenge, then the essays in this volume do, I believe, meet it well. The second problem is the extent to which these essays reveal some common factor and unity of purpose. At first glance, the broad range of topics appears to suggest no such unifying principle. But the impression is not entirely accurate, for all the essays do have in common the purpose of examining, from quite different points of view, either Shaw's skill as a dramatist or his relationship to a tradition of ideas that contributed to the shaping of his dramatic technique.

In some of the criticism in this collection there is an analysis of both the shaping ideas and the playwright's skill. The first essay, for example, written by Alan Downer, explores Shaw's dramaturgical principles through what would currently be called "historical" and "new critical" techniques. Shaw, according to Downer, collaborated with William Archer on an unfinished play called *Rheingold*. It subsequently became *Widowers' Houses*, Shaw's first produced play. Obviously, the "historical" method is being used in this kind of investigation, but the essay also includes, without any reference to outside material, a close and careful examination of Shaw's dramatic method. Even for those who favour neither the extrinsic nor the intrinsic approach but prefer critical analysis that perceives and describes large thematic patterns running throughout the corpus of a playwright's work, Downer's essay will not be disappointing.

The second essay, by Stanley Weintraub, deals with the genesis of *Man and Superman*. Unlike Downer's approach, Weintraub's examination relies almost exclusively on material and events preceding the production of *Man and Superman*. The essay traces the growth of the play's form and content through Shaw's experience with several genres: dramatic criticism, drama, the short story, and the socialist novel. The result, Weintraub insists, is "one of the century's great plays."

Although concerned primarily with Somerset Maugham's play, *The Circle* (performed along with two Shaw plays at the Shaw Festival's 1967 season), Brian Parker's paper points out contrasts between Shaw and Maugham, "largely in Shaw's favour," that "clarify the qualities that are peculiarly Maugham's." Of particular interest is Maugham's opinion, obviously arising from some irritation with Shaw's box-office success, that Shaw's ideas lacked originality and that Shaw's popularity arose from his tendency to pander to "the English audiences' fascinated distrust of sexual passion." But the essay also stands on its own merits as an incisive and clear analysis of an often overlooked dramatist's treatment of the clash between instinct and society.

The problem of Shaw's ideas and their origins is the topic of the essay by Warren Smith, who analyzes Shaw's debt to the numerous societies to which he belonged. The evidence that Smith amasses leaves no room for disputing the view that Shaw was indeed a joiner. The joining, however, was no mere superficial way to pass time. Smith believes that Shaw's involvement with these various groups had an important effect on Shaw: "In these same decades the diffident young Dubliner, George B. Shaw, went through the crucible of London art galleries, music halls, theatres, lecture halls, editorial rooms, libraries, committee rooms, outdoor meetings, and ladies' boudoirs to emerge as the delicately adjusted schizophrenic prophet-jokester, Bernard Shaw-GBS."

Similar to the essays dealing mainly with outside influences on Shaw is James Merritt's essay on Shaw and the pre-Raphaelites. Merritt outlines the historical background of the Pre-Raphaelite Movement and proceeds to point out the characteristics of the Movement that influenced Shaw and where they surface again in his drama. Merritt goes so far as to suggest (with convincing evidence, too) that the Movement provided characteristics that are reflected in Shaw's *Candida* to the extent that the play might possibly be seen as "an allegory of pre-Raphaelitism."

Clifford Leech's essay, "Shaw and Shakespeare," is important for the light it casts on two problems frequently associated with Shaw's dramas. The first is whether Shaw's plays are dated, or, to put it another way, will Shaw's plays last. Leech's analysis is based not only on duration – Shaw has "lasted" for nearly three-quarters of a century – but also on the criterion of literary merit. What he finds in Shaw's drama is the work of a dramatist who explores the permanent and perennial problems that humanity faces in every age. The point about pleasing long is examined in conjunction with the second problem: Shaw's merit in comparison with other playwrights, particularly Shakespeare. Leech's essay avoids the clichés usually associated with such a comparison and succeeds in focusing on the dramatic modes in which each dramatist achieved his fullest artistry: tragedy for Shakespeare and argumentative comedy for Shaw. Refreshingly enough, Leech's conclusion makes no extravagant claims and awards no ribbons for undying superiority. One of his conclusions, simply but carefully arrived at, is that "Shaw believed in argument, but Shakespeare did not."

The last essay, by Martin Meisel, deals with the relationship between Shaw's plays and his political thinking. One aspect of this relationship is the highly relevant problem of violent revolution. What Meisel finds in Shaw's drama, particularly in *Heartbreak House*, is a strategy designed to "culminate in a state of feeling, often including uneasiness and unresolved stress, that will effect a permanent change in consciousness bearing on social change." The various methods for bringing about that change are the subject of much of Meisel's discussion. Perhaps the most fascinating section of this essay is the analysis of the imagery Shaw chose in order to dramatize the apocalypse in *Heartbreak House*, *On the Rocks*, *The Simpleton of the Unexpected Isles*, and *Geneva*. The discussion of images of the apocalypse, although vitally related to the idea of revolution, also leads Meisel to an examination of Shaw's political essays and the specific differences between the plays and the essays. He reaches the conclusion that from *Heartbreak House* on there is no discrepancy between Shaw's plays and his politics.

Besides the two problems mentioned earlier in this introduction there is also the question of the relevance of these essays to current Shavian criticism. An answer to that is not easily formulated, simply because current Shavian criticism focuses on a range of topics that is as wide as Shaw's own interests and work. A glance at other collections of critical essays reveals that Shaw has engaged scholars whose approaches and subject matter are as various as Shaw's achievements. It is, therefore, difficult to detect a mainstream of Shavian criticism. This state is not a lamentable one, for it surely indicates an attempt to reinterpret Shaw for modern audiences. This effort is in itself a tribute to a playwright who might conceivably speak to an audience that is yet unborn.

N.R.

Shaw: Seven Critical Essays

ALAN S. DOWNER

Shaw's First Play

The title of this lecture really should have been *Shaw's First Plays*, though that would have been as ambiguous as the present one. It is reasonably common knowledge that Shaw's first produced play was *Widowers' Houses*, but *Widowers' Houses* is only preliminary to my central concern; *Getting Married* was, by his own calculation, Shaw's seventeenth play, but it was the first that was from start to finish pure Shaw. In *Getting Married* his dramaturgical principles are most purely displayed, the structure and techniques of this play distinguishing the Shavian play from the Pinerotic or Ibsene.

Shaw himself was never at a loss for ways to explain how he differed from his fellows. To the Joint Select Parliamentary committee on censorship he introduced himself in the following uningratiating manner: "I am by profession a playwright. I have been in practice since 1892. ... I am not an ordinary playwright in general practice. I am a specialist in immoral and heretical plays,"[1] G.B.S., M.D. In *Back to Methuselah* he portrays himself as The Elderly Gentleman who dies of discouragement because he is unable to join the Long-Livers or to tolerate any longer the lie-directed life of his fellow Short-Livers. In his great chronicle history play, one may be pardoned for seeing still a different self-portrait in the armoured heroine who cries into the spotlight at its close, "Oh Lord that madest this beautiful earth, when will it be ready to receive thy *saints*?" But most often he saw himself as the gadfly: the mountebank selling his subversive doctrines from a cart in Hyde Park, the circus clown cheeking the ringmaster. The special Shavian conceit of clownage is in that word "cheeking": his clown is not the figure so familiar to us, with the electrified nose and papier-maché feet or the sad-faced Joey. His conceit is not to blow himself up in a midget automobile, but to debag the symbol of institutionalized authority that the spectators may perceive beneath the uniform of superiority a bare forked animal no better, no wiser, no more sacred than themselves. In his bag of tricks this clown must have two specialized and incompatible items, a bundle of nonconformist ideas and a complete set of the dramatic conventions acceptable to the audiences of his day, but manufactured out of instantly reversible material.

How the clown became a playwright is an oft-told tale, but it is both pertinent to my subject and too good not to tell again. In 1884, William Archer, drama critic and translator of Ibsen, encountered Shaw, novelist and critic of art and music, seated at a desk in the British Museum simultaneously reading a French translation of *Das Kapital* and the score of *Tristan und Isolde*. Shortly thereafter Archer suggested – in all innocence – that they collaborate on the writing of a drama, Archer to provide the scenario and Shaw the dialogue. What Archer may have had in mind can be hypothesized from his one occasionally remembered drama, *The Green Goddess*, in which a selection of British aristocrats are to be executed by a villainous rajah when the sun's rays pass over a religious idol. Shaw seems to have had nothing in particular in mind, except that he was not much pleased with the proposed title of the play: *Rheingold*. In a short time, Archer produced the scenario, more or less stolen according to custom from a Parisian success. Shaw worked on the project in his spare moments, of which there were not many since the off hours when he was not earning his living by journalism were given like those of the Rev. James Mavor Morell to speaking for every cause that could in the slightest way engage his gadfly instinct. In October of 1887 he deposited two acts of *Rheingold* with Archer, describing them in an accompanying note as "a series of consecutive dialogues in which your idea is prepared and developed." But he complains about the scenario: "I don't see how the long lost old woman is to be introduced without destroying the realism and freshness of the play: she would simply turn the thing into a plot, and ruin it." And he has exhausted Archer's entire scenario on the first two acts. "I think the story will bear four acts; but I have no idea of how it is to proceed. ... Will you proceed either to chuck in the remaining acts, or provide me with a skeleton for them? You will perceive that my genius has brought the romantic notion which possessed you, into vivid contact with real life."[2]

There are certain keys to the quintessence of Shavianism in that early note: a series of consecutive dialogues in which an idea is prepared and developed; no idea of how the action will proceed beyond the point reached; a plot spells ruin for a play; a romantic notion brought into contact with real life. But Archer never understood Shaw. He heard the first act with contempt and went to sleep in the middle of the second.[3] Shaw abandoned the project. Our story thus assumes the conventional structure of the well-made play; the first act is exposition, laying the ground work for future action, and the act drop falls on the unspoken question of what will happen next. Suspense.

One version of the next act of the Clown's Conversion to Playwright begins with the entrance of J. T. Grein. The mere fact that Grein was an actual man and not an invention supports Shaw's contention that his dramatic work is based upon natural history, scientifically observed, for Grein could very well have been a Shavian invention. A native of Holland, he made his living in part by translating English novels into Dutch. And with the money earned from translating Mrs. Burnett's milk-and-honey *Little Lord Fauntleroy* he performed the Shavian act of staging the first English production of Ibsen's *Ghosts*. The storm of vituperation that was visited upon him for his attempt to introduce the English theatre-going public to their own century could hardly have been more violent if he had attempted to assassinate the Queen. Nor, considering him as a typical Shavian hero, could it have given him greater encouragement for further quixotic adventures. He next determined to find a native playwright willing to seize the torch from Ibsen. There are at least two accounts of what happened next and they are equally illuminating in different ways. The first comes from one of Grein's associates. In search of an English playwright, he says, Grein scanned the literary landscape of the day until his eye chanced to light on George Bernard Shaw, gaunt, red bearded, and looking like an untamed wolf. Since he seemed unapproachable, it was necessary to devise a plan for approaching him. The way to approach an egocentric, original thinker, they decided, was to persuade him that as a man they considered him greater than Caesar or Napoleon and as a writer, greater than Milton or Shakespeare; once you have persuaded him of this, you can get him to do anything you want. Of course he does not like flattery, but then he does not know you are flattering him: he only thinks you are unusually perceptive and judicious. Having determined on their plan, they acted, and Shaw picked up his cues without hesitation. The two carefully preserved acts of the unfinished *Rheingold* were removed from his files and under Grein's encouragement completed and produced as *Widowers' Houses*. By this time, said Grein's associate, Shaw was persuaded that he had discovered them, not they him, and "no doubt thinks so still."[4]

The other account is Shaw's own, and must be told in his words:

> [The Independent Theatre] got on its feet by producing Ibsen's *Ghosts*; but its search for unacted native dramatic masterpieces ... was so complete a failure that at the end of 1892 it had not produced a single original piece of any magnitude by an English author. In this humiliating national emergency, I proposed to Mr. Grein that he should boldly announce a play by me. Being an extraordinarily sanguine and enterprising man, he took this step without hesitation. I then raked out, from my dustiest pile

> of discarded and rejected manuscripts, two acts of a play I had begun in 1885, shortly after the close of my novel writing period, in collaboration with my friend William Archer. ... I completed it by a third act; gave it the farfetched Scriptural title of "Widowers' Houses"; and handed it over to Mr. Grein, who launched it at the public. ... It made a sensation out of all proportion to its merits or even its demerits; and I at once became infamous as a playwright.[5]

Which version contains the greater part of truth does not matter, for both have something to add to the quintessence of Shavianism: the independent original thinker rising like Shiprock out of the surrounding desert, monumental, but scalable; the artist who measures his success by the extent to which his audience is shocked. The curtain of our second act falls upon the author standing behind the footlights of the Royalty Theatre and bowing with equal satisfaction to the applause from one part of his audience and to the boos from the other.

For the third act of the Clown's Conversion we must look briefly at *Widowers' Houses* itself and somewhat more carefully at its aftermath. There is certainly nothing in the opening of *Widowers' Houses* to disturb an audience that had come in search of a romanticized version of the daily round of eating, drinking, and giving in marriage. The setting is the garden restaurant of a resort hotel on the Rhine and the first characters to enter are two Englishmen on vacation – a somewhat unkempt boyish hero named Trench and Charles-his-friend, named in this instance Cokane. From the exposition we learn that they have observed on the steamer a charming English maiden and her formidable papa. Enter, in the approved theatrical manner, charming young maiden and formidable papa, Mr. Sartorius. The young lady is not quite what we, as members of the London audience in 1892, might have expected. She is described as "well-dressed, well-fed, good-looking, strong minded ... none the worse for being vital and energetic rather than delicate and refined." That is, she is not one of the Dickensian heroines, but one of those New Women, the Unwomanly Women, that Shaw had discovered in Ibsen. Her name is Blanche and in herself and in the light of Shaw's future development she is quite the most taking thing in a not very taking play. There follows a brief comedy of manners in which the hero's friend and the heroine's father manage to become acquainted without any breach of the rigorous decorum that governs Englishmen on tour, and thus the hero and heroine are introduced to one another with full consideration of the proprieties. But when father and friend have left the stage, we discover that the young couple had already progressed to a rather startling degree of intimacy on their own initiative while on board the steamer. More startling still, the initiative seems to be the heroine's.

Trench Blanche. (*She bristles instantly; overdoes it; and frightens him*). I beg your pardon for calling you by your name; but I – er – (*She corrects her mistake by softening her expression eloquently. He responds with a gush*) You *don't* mind do you? I felt sure you wouldn't, somehow. Well, look here. I have no idea how you will receive this: it must seem horribly abrupt; but the circumstances do not admit of – the fact is, my utter want of tact – (*he flounders more and more, unable to see that she can scarcely contain her eagerness*). Now, if it were Cokane –
Blanche (*impatiently*) Cokane!
Trench (*terrified*) No, not Cokane. Though I assure you I was only going to say about him that –
Blanche That he will be back presently with papa.
Trench (*stupidly*) Yes: they can't be very long now. I hope I'm not detaining you.
Blanche I thought you were detaining me because you had something to say.
Trench (*totally unnerved*) Not at all. At least, nothing very particular. That is, I'm afraid you wouldn't think it very particular. Another time, perhaps –
Blanche What other time? How do you know that we shall ever meet again? (*Desperately*) Tell me now. I *want* you to tell me now.
Trench Well, I was thinking that if we could make up our minds to – or not to – at least – er – (*His nervousness deprives him of the power of speech*).

Blanche (*giving him up as hopeless*) I don't think there's much danger of *your* making up *your* mind, Dr. Trench.
Trench (*stammering*) I only thought – (*He stops and looks at her piteously. She hesitates a moment, and then puts her hands into his with calculated impulsiveness. He snatches her into his arms with a cry of relief*) Dear Blanche! I thought I should never have said it. I believe I should have stood stuttering here all day if you hadn't helped me out with it.
Blanche (*indignantly trying to break loose from him*) I didn't help you out with it.
Trench (*holding her*) I don't mean that you did it on purpose, of course. Only instinctively.
Blanche (*still a little anxious*) But you haven't said anything.
Trench What more can I say than this? (*He kisses her again*).
Blanche (*overcome by the kiss, but holding on to her point*) But Harry –
Trench (*delighted at the name*) Yes.
Blanche When shall we be married?

In the three or four minutes of dialogue between Trench and Blanche is the germ of the entire comedy of *Man and Superman* and in Blanche, the heroine who quite literally takes matters into her own hands, is the progenitrix not only of Vivie Warren and Anne Whitefield, but of Zoo, and Joan, and any other heroine whose place is not usurped by the master himself imperfectly disguised in a toga or a ship captain's uniform. That Blanche is pure Shaw is clear from the fact that you can search in vain for her counterpart in the works of his fellow playwrights. Only in *The Importance of Being Earnest*, that gallery of strong-minded women, are her equals to be found, accounting perhaps for Oscar Wilde's statement that *Widowers' Houses* showed Shaw's "superb confidence in the dramatic values of the mere facts of life."[6]

The wooing scene having established the true relationship of the lovers, the action of *Widowers' Houses* proceeds with the re-entrance of Cokane and Sartorius who have, of course, seen what they were not supposed to see, the embrace. This entrance is of a piece with the earlier entrance of Blanche and her papa, at the moment most opportune for advancing the action of the play, regardless of logic or the timetables by which people outside of plays conduct their business. The unwarranted or unexpected entrance was a staple of popular drama, whose governing principle was to move forward at all costs; Shaw adopts it with the instincts of a debater whose aim is to keep an argument going until it exhausts itself. And here once again as in his treatment of the conventional heroine Shaw departs from the expectations aroused by the theatrical form he has chosen. The well-made play was plotted backwards so that every event, however startling, would on examination prove to have been meticulously prepared for; and so, doubtless, was the scenario that Archer had drawn up. But the formidable papa, discovering his daughter in the arms of a young man she has apparently just met, reacts in a totally unexpected fashion: Trench can have his daughter if Trench can promise that Sartorius and Blanche will be accepted as equals by Trench's family. This reversal of the conventions of middle-class respectability leads to a passage of comic invention which might have come straight from *Box and Cox*, the classic of Victorian farce. Trench agrees to write to his family, describing his prospective father-in-law and inquiring about his acceptability. Being, as we have seen, something less than articulate, he requests that Cokane draft the letter. Cokane agrees and is left alone to make several false starts. At this point, Sartorius appears, makes a few inquiries and a few suggestions and ultimately dictates the letter which can only create the suspenseful question of what *can* happen next?

The audience could hardly have been prepared for the sequel, for one of the things never discussed in polite drama was where, except in the case of demi-mondaines, the characters derived their apparently unearned incomes (even the hero or the heroine on the verge of destitution would be rescued by marriage to a partner of unlimited and unexplained means). What happens next in *Widowers' Houses* is the revelation that Sartorius is a slum landlord and, although acceptable to Trench's family, unacceptable to Trench who is both an idealist and a doctor of medicine. (Shaw would drop that combination.) He will still marry Blanche, but she must come to him without her father's tainted money. The proposal strikes his fiancée as preposterous, particularly when it is revealed that Trench's income derives from a mortgage on the slum landlord's property. One must be scrupulously fair to the young hero: he had never inquired from whence his money came and he is too stunned by the revelation to make the properly heroic renunciation. But, again an unheralded and unexpected turn of events: Blanche refuses to go with her idealistic sweetheart and elects to remain an old maid at the hearth of the paternal rent-gouger.

The Greeks, as usual, had a word for this reversal, *peripeteia.* In their serious drama the peripeteia was the climactic moment of the action when the hero made the final discovery about himself or his situation which resulted in the complete reversal of his fortunes. What was climactic in serious drama became a general structural principle in comedy. For Menander, for Plautus, for Terence, for the scenarists of the *commedia dell'arte*, the peripeteia became a way of keeping the play alive; their dramaturgy was the art of devising as many turns as possible to involve the characters in a series of unresolved dilemmas until invention flagged and some sort of accommodation was allowed to occur. Victorian farce employed, above all things, peripeteia. Box is a printer who works by night, Cox is a hatter who works by day. Mrs. Bouncer is the landlady who has rented the same room to both men, having persuaded herself that they will never be in residence during the same hours. Cox departs for his day at the hat shop, Box returns from his night's work and begins to prepare his bedtime snack. As Box leaves the room for a moment, Cox enters rejoicing that he has been given the day off (turn). When he discovers a rasher frying in *his* pan over *his* fire he suspects that Mrs. Bouncer is taking advantage of his absence, throws the bacon out the window and replaces it with a chop he has purchased for breakfast. Then *he* departs for a moment and (turn) Box re-enters and the whole routine is repeated. The play is still very funny in the theatre, but farce makes bad retelling; suffice it that peripeteia follows peripeteia as the two men meet, fall out (turn), fall in (turn), unite against Bouncer (turn), discover that they have both been engaged to the same woman (turn), discover that each has faked a suicide to escape from her clutches (turn), are informed that she has uncovered the truth and is coming to claim her beloved, vie with one another in unselfish resignation of their claims (turn). Enter Mrs. Bouncer with the message that the young lady has changed her mind and has married someone else (turn). Box fixes Cox with a sudden suspicious glance. "Have you," he inquires, "a strawberry mark on your left arm?" Cox after a moment's thought answers, "No." Box draws back, "Brother!" he cries, they rush into each other's arms, and the curtain calls a halt to peripeteia. *Box and Cox* is the sheerest, purposeless foolery and its life depends wholly on the skill of the playwright in devising situations that can lead to one reversal after another.[7]

It was a dramaturgical device that Shaw adopted with delight and adapted with skill to his own purposes. When he complained to Archer that a plot would ruin a play, he was declaring his own boredom with formulaic cause and effect, with the doctrine of Dumas *fils* that the art of the drama was the art of preparation, just as he had finally rejected the novel form as too clumsy and unreal. In the years between *Rheingold* and *Widowers' Houses* he had written to a correspondent: "Sometimes in spare moments I write dialogues; and these are all working up to a certain end (a sermon of course) my imagination playing the usual tricks meanwhile of creating visionary persons, etc. When I have a few hundred of these dialogues worked up and interlocked, then a drama will be the result – a moral, instructive, suggestive comedy of modern society, guaranteed correct in philosophic and economic detail, and unactably independent of theatrical considerations."[8] By means of a series of reversals common in Victorian farce Shaw was able to get from dialogue to dialogue without wasting energy on vraisemblance, logistics, or the moving finger of time.

Shaw, then, by reshaping the materials that stood ready to his hand, begins to establish his own brand of drama in his maiden work. His characters are familiar: nubile maiden, idealist hero, stern parent; but their behaviour is unexpected. The sweet young thing hauls her maid about the stage by the hair of her head, takes the initiative in the love scenes, and finally seduces the hero into accepting the profits of slum landlordism. The idealist hero cannot bring himself to surrender his income for his ideals and is, in the end, no unwilling victim of the heroine's far-from-moral suasion. The rent-gouging stern parent is granted his own "dialogue," and since it complicates the hero's position through the unfamiliar dramatic subject of economics rather than morals, patriotism, or sex, it becomes one more element in what might be called Shaw's bloodless dramatic revolution.

As the second act of *Widowers' Houses* approaches its climax, Trench announces to his future father-in-law that he is determined to take nothing from him but Blanche herself. When Sartorius accuses him of indecision, he explains that he did not know whence Sartorius derived his income.

> *Sartorius* (*outraged*) Sir! (They confront one another threateningly.)
> *Cokane* (*softly*) Rent must be paid, dear boy. It is inevitable, Harry, inevitable. (*Trench turns away petulantly. Sartorius looks after him reflectively for a moment; then resumes his former deliberate and dignified manner, and addresses Trench with studied consideration, but with a perceptible condescension to his youth and folly.*)
> *Sartorius* I am afraid, Dr. Trench, that you are a very young hand at business; and I am sorry I forgot that for a moment or so. May I ask you to suspend your judgement until we have had a little quiet discussion of this sentimental notion of yours? if you will excuse me for calling it so. ...
> *Trench* I have no objection to sit down and listen; but I don't see how that can make black white. ...

Sartorius I assume, to begin with, Dr. Trench, that you are not a Socialist, or anything of that sort.
Trench Certainly not. I'm a Conservative. At least, if I ever took the trouble to vote, I should vote for the Conservative and against the other fellow. ...
Sartorius I am glad to find that so far we are in perfect sympathy. I am, of course, a Conservative. Not a narrow or prejudiced one, I hope, nor at all opposed to true progress. Still, a sound Conservative ... As to my business, it is simply to provide homes suited to the small means of very poor people, who require roofs to shelter them just like other people. Do you suppose I can keep up those roofs for nothing?
Trench Yes: that's all very fine; but the point is, what sort of homes do you give them for their money? People must live somewhere, or else go to jail. Advantage is taken of that to make them pay for houses that are not fit for dogs. Why don't you build proper dwellings, and give fair value for the money you take?
Sartorius (*pitying his innocence*) My young friend: these poor people do not know how to live in proper dwellings: they would wreck them in a week. You doubt me: try it for yourself. You are welcome to replace all the missing banisters, handrails, cistern lids and dusthole tops at your own expense; and you will find them missing again in less than three days: burnt, sir, every stick of them. I do not blame the poor creatures: they need fires, and often have no other way of getting them. But I really cannot spend pound after pound in repairs for them to pull down, when I can barely get them to pay me four and sixpence a week for a room, which is recognized fair London rent. No, gentlemen: when people are very poor, you *cannot* help them, no matter how much you may sympathize with them. It does them more harm than good in the long run. ... And now, Dr. Trench, may I ask what *your* income is derived from?

Shaw is willing to endow the enemies of society with enough of his own rhetorical powers to make their ounce of self-justification hold up against a deal of socialist theory, in this instance to keep Trench at arm's length until the enemy is in position to move in for the kill. Given time, Trench might have countered Sartorius with arguments of his own, but once he knows the answer to that final question he can only protest, "Do you mean to say that I am just as bad as you are?" To which Sartorius replies: "If, when you say you are just as bad as I am, you mean that you are just as powerless to alter the state of society, then you are unfortunately quite right."

Such dialogues, which become more extended and more intricate in the later plays and not infrequently rise into monologues of superb eloquence, must share the blame with the notorious prefaces for the popular image of Shaw as thinker rather than playwright. But if *Widowers' Houses* has any vitality today it is certainly not because it advocates low-income housing any more than Ibsen's reputation depends on his propagandizing for sanitary engineering. The profession of slum landlord is a dramatic metaphor, like Mrs. Warren's profession. The audience is not merely to reprobate landlord or bawd, but to experience its own part in the metaphor. Some years later Shaw explained to a young critic that *Widowers' Houses* was "what people call realistic" but that his own purpose in writing it "was to make people thoroughly uncomfortable whilst entertaining them artistically."[9] All in all, it was, as he said, recalling the audience reaction, "a promising failure."[10]

Widowers' Houses was a failure because, in spite of the omission of the long-lost old lady, it is bound by a plot of sorts and because audiences were not yet ready for its Shavian elements; but it is promising because its author proved to himself that he could create a vehicle that would perform its assigned functions, the prototype of Shavian drama.

A word about Shavian may not be amiss. Early in his career, he used occasionally to refer to his ideas or his style with the awkward epithet Shawian. Sydney Cockerell, then secretary to William Morris, told him the story of an English classical scholar named Shaw who eagerly searched in a new German edition of a Greek or Latin text for references to some emendations he had proposed. At last he came upon quite a long passage in a footnote, followed by the words: *sic shavius-sed inepte*. Shaw immediately adopted the epithet for himself, and forced the qualifying clause to eat its own words. The Shavian drama, which first appears in uncorrupted form as the third act of *Man and Superman*, constitutes the entire design of *Getting Married* and *Misalliance*, then forms an easy partnership with more familiar theatrical forms in *Heartbreak House* and *St. Joan*, and reaches its final highly individual expression in *In Good King Charles's Golden Days*, one of the triumphs of the modern dramatic repertory.

Getting Married was the first completely Shavian play. It is in one long uninterrupted act. There is no plot in the sense of a conventionally patterned action requiring the devising of incidents to permit suspenseful curtains. It is instead a series of dialogues hinged together by peripeteias, which are more often than not the unexpected and unexplained entrance of the character least welcome and most likely to irritate the debaters or to upset the point they are about to agree upon. To be sure, the subject is wooing and wedding, which Shaw felt was an unreasonable waste of an audience's time, but the question is not who, or which, but whether and on what grounds; it is not a question of romance, or propriety, but of the social contract. Shaw's marital comedy is related not so much to *As You Like It* as to *The Way of the World* and its action exhausts the possibilities of the proviso scene.

The setting is the palace of the Bishop of Chelsea, specifically his spacious eleventh century kitchen. If there is a dramatic reason for choosing the kitchen rather than the parlor, study, or bedroom for a discussion of the nature of marriage, it may be that the kitchen is the seat of domestic economy, while the other rooms house activities less central to Shaw's main concern. In this kitchen assemble the characters, most of them members of a large and, as one of them says, "pretty typical" English family, to turn over every stone between the wedding altar and the marriage bed. It is part of Shaw's purpose that we should recognize them, first as familiar theatrical types, then, as he delicately removes their conventional masks, as our friends and neighbours and ourselves. The problem is not whether Cecil Sykes will marry Edith Bridgenorth, but how any personal relationship can be maintained in a society calculated to enslave and debase the individual. As if to emphasize this, one conventional character is missing: Hymen, the marriage-broker of the gods. In the whole play there is no one to ease our consciences with the comfortable declaration that

> there is mirth in heaven
> When earthly things made even
> Atone together.

The play begins on the wedding morning of Edith Bridgenorth and Cecil Sykes. Mrs. Bridgenorth, wife of the Bishop and mother of the bride-to-be, is discussing arrangements with Collins, the local greengrocer who has been in charge of three earlier weddings of Bridgenorth daughters. Collins is another of Shaw's variations on the clever servant, like the Waiter in *You Never Can Tell* or Bluntschli in *Arms and the Man*, the common man who can manage anything because he is not restricted by the regulations of class or office. To them enters General Bridgenorth, the Bishop's brother, the Shavian *miles ingloriosus*. His job is to give away the last of his nieces, but the occasion like each of its predecessors fills him with anguish, for he is hopelessly in love with Lesbia Grantham who has for twenty years turned a deaf ear to his wooing. Lesbia, we are to learn, is devoted to children and would make an ideal mother, but she cannot tolerate the continuous presence of a man; further, as she declares, she is an English lady and has been trained to do without what she cannot have on honourable terms, no matter what it is. The Bishop's other brother Reginald, who has just been through a sordid divorce, is the next to appear, a middle-aged adolescent. Both Mrs. Bridgenorth and the General resent his presence and demand that he leave. They are very fond of Leo, the wife who had divorced him, and distressed at what she might feel if she were to come in and find him there. Of course, at that moment, Leo does come in. In our day, Leo might have been a member of Miss McCarthy's Vassar group; she is the sweet girl graduate, knowing the biggest name for everything but incapable of understanding anything. To everyone's surprise, except Shaw's, we learn that Reginald, the apparent rotter, had consented to go off to Brighton with a hired correspondent (who promptly fell in love with him) in order that Leo might marry St. John Hotchkiss – who is to be the best man at the day's wedding. Shaw wastes no time in getting St. John into the kitchen to introduce the central problem of the play.

Cecil, it seems, that morning received a volume of essays on *Men's Wrongs* pointing out that the husband is legally responsible if his wife should libel someone in public, a charge which his estate could not bear. And since Edith is a bishop's daughter she is active in social causes: "When her blood boils about it (and it boils at least once a week) she doesn't care what she says." Cecil is rightly reluctant to enter upon so precarious a future. He has no more than stated his fears when his fiancée enters with a pamphlet *she* has received in the mail: DO YOU KNOW WHAT YOU ARE GOING TO DO? BY A WOMAN WHO HAS DONE IT. What the authoress had done was to marry a man who, three children later, committed murder and was imprisoned for life. Since he had only committed murder and not adultery she was unable to divorce him. The lesson is not lost upon Edith; she will not enter upon so uncompromising a future. Hotchkiss, whose entrance had introduced the problem, now advances a proposed solution. "Let us," he suggests, "draw up the first English partnership deed." The Bishop is the first to agree, and then Lesbia, who declares that if honourable conditions can be devised she is willing to enter into an alliance with the General.

Seeking assistance they turn to Collins as businessman and alderman. The idea of a contract between members of the same class strikes him as such a novelty that he feels he must consult his sister-in-law, the lady mayoress, who is given to trances and whose husband has been most tolerant of her need for variety in her relationship with men.

The Bishop now remembers his chaplain, Soames, who had given up a successful law practice for the life of a celibate priest. As a convert, Father Anthony is a good deal more rigorous than his bishop; his advice to all is to do their duty by taking the Christian vows of celibacy and poverty, but as a dutiful chaplain he awaits their instructions about the contract.

Reginald We got stuck on the first clause. What should we begin with?
Soames It is usual to begin with the term of the contract.
Edith What does that mean?
Soames The term of years for which it is to hold good.
Leo But this is a marriage contract.
Soames Is the marriage to be for a year, a week, or a day?
Reginald Come, I say, Anthony! You're worse than any of us. A day!
Soames Off the path is off the path. An inch or a mile: what does it matter?
Leo If the marriage is not to be for ever, I'll have nothing to do with it. I call it immoral to have a marriage for a term of years. If the people don't like it they can get divorced.

And so it goes. A proposal is made only to be overturned by the next speaker, while Soames's dry legalisms make a mockery of the efforts of flesh and blood to arrive at an accommodation satisfactory to a variety of individual needs. The Bishop, meanwhile, quietly stands by or occasionally encourages the proponents to develop their views at greater length, knowing the Shavian doctrine that if you give the devil fair play, he loses his case. Since no one can agree on a single point Soames puts an end to the argument by tearing the much-blotted draft of the contract. Marriage as an institution cannot be humanized by recourse to the institution of law.

Soames's gesture is the cue for the entrance of Mrs. George, the lady mayoress, and one of Shaw's most original creations. A woman of the people (the mayor is a coal merchant), an adventuress, she wears her authority with grace and assurance. She is the *ewig weibliche*, endlessly fascinating to men (St. John instantly follows her like a puppy) and so demanding that her exhausted lovers return her to her husband within a day or two. Also, having been for many years a devoted listener to the Bishop's sermons, she is Innamorata Apascionata, authoress of pseudonymous love letters to the Bishop intended to prepare the way for their eventual assignation in heaven. Most of the rest of the play belongs to her as she spars with the ladies and fences with the men using the weapons of vulgar sense and the wisdom of the earth. Finally, alone with the Bishop and his chaplain she falls into a trance and speaks with the voice of the Life Force, which – as always in Shaw – sounds a little like the King James Bible read with just a trace of a Protestant Irish lilt.

> *Mrs. George* I have earned the right to speak. I have dared: I have gone through: I have not fallen withered in the fire: I have come at last out beyond, to the back of Godspeed.
> *The Bishop* And what do you see there, at the back of Godspeed?
> *Soames* [hungrily] Give us your message.
> *Mrs. George* [with intensely sad reproach]. When you loved me I gave you the whole sun and stars to play with. I gave you eternity in a single moment, strength of the mountains in one clasp of your arms, and the volume of all the seas in one impulse of your souls. A moment only; but was it not enough? Were you not paid then for all the rest of your struggle on earth? Must I mend your clothes and sweep your floors as well? Was it not enough? I paid the price without bargaining: I bore the children without flinching: was that a reason for heaping fresh burdens on me? I carried the child in my arms: must I carry the father too? When I opened the gates of paradise, were you blind? was it nothing to you? When all the stars sang in your ears and all the winds swept you into the heart of heaven, were you deaf? were you dull? was I no more to you than a bone to a dog? Was it not enough? We spent eternity together; and you ask me for a little lifetime more. We possessed all the universe together; and you ask me to give you my scanty wages as well. I have given you the greatest of all things; and you ask me to give you

little things. I gave you your own soul: you ask me for my body as a plaything. Was it not enough? Was it not enough?

After paradox and peripeteia, legalism and mysticism – the solution. The other members of the family return to announce that Cecil and Edith have solved their problem and have been married in a civil ceremony. They have resorted to the simple expedient on the one hand of a policy insuring Cecil against libel actions brought on account of anything Edith might say, and on the other, Cecil's solemn vow that if he ever should commit a crime he will also knock her down before a witness and go off to Brighton with another lady. As for the Reginald-Leo-St. John triangle, St. John discovers that he prefers the Earth Mother, Lady Mayoress, to Leo, the blue stocking, and Leo sends Reginald to get their divorce annulled. Only Lesbia holds out, "a glorious strong-minded old maid of old England." The lady mayoress agrees that St. John may hang about her house as a source of conversation and amusement.

St. John You may take me home with you. ... You have nothing to fear.
Mayoress And nothing to hope?
St. John Since you put it in that more than kind way ... absolutely nothing.
Mayoress Ha! Like most men, you think you know everything a woman wants, don't you? But the thing one wants most has nothing to do with marriage at all.

Soames suggests that the thing is "Christian fellowship."

Mayoress You call it that, do you?
Soames What do you call it?

But we never learn what it is, for this is the end of the play. One of Shaw's old sweethearts said, late in life, that he never had the gift of sympathetic penetration into a woman's nature: "He employs his clever detective powers and pounces on weaknesses and faults which confirm his preconceived ideas. He imagines he understands."[11] To put it another way, *Getting*

Married shows that Shaw knows practically everything about marriage and nothing whatever about love – to which he might properly reply, as to Archer in the beginning, that he had brought our romantic notions in contact with real life, that is, with economics and sociology.

Getting Married is pure Shavianism: a drama made up of the conflict of ideas or principles (mostly unthought-upon or irrational) which stand in the way of the functioning of the Life Force and establishing a social contract which will permit its fullest realization. *Sic shavius-sed inepte.* Later, with more regard for the capacities of his audience, he will moderate his rigorous Shavianism with the more comfortable elements of time, place, and something like a conventional dramatic action to create *Heartbreak House*, *St. Joan*, and *Back to Methuselah*, the three masterworks of his dramatic creativity. But there was nothing accidental or whimsical about his venture into pure Shavianism. Shaw was as self-conscious about his art as about his own public image.

At about the time he was working on *Getting Married*, Shaw advanced some thoughts on dramaturgy which may serve as a summary of the principles of Shavian drama. Ostensibly, he is writing in praise of his French contemporary, Brieux, but he had already remade Ibsen in his own image, and if the greater, why not the lesser dramatist?

First, as to the matter of plot:

> No writer of the first order needs the formula [of the well made play] any more than a sound man needs a crutch. ... He finds no difficulty in setting people on the stage to talk and act in an amusing, exciting or touching way. His characters have adventures and ideas which are interesting in themselves, and need not be fitted into the Chinese puzzle of a plot.[12]

Second, as to the function of the playwright:

> [it is] to pick out the significant incidents from the chaos of daily happenings and arrange them so that their relationship to one another becomes significant, thus changing us from bewildered

> spectators of a monstrous confusion to men intelligently conscious of the world and its destinies. This is the highest function that man can perform.[13]

Third, the method of the playwright:

> [he must] attack and destroy [accepted formulae for playwriting because the public must be taught that] the romantic conventions on which the formula proceeds are all false. [He can do nothing with his audiences] until he has cured them of looking at the stage as through a keyhole, and sniffing round the theatre as prurient people sniff round the divorce court.[14]

Fourth, as to subject matter:

> To ask an audience to spend three hours hanging on the question of which particular man some particular woman shall mate with does not strike [the serious playwright] as a reasonable proceeding.[15] [Rather, he will devote himself to] that kind of comedy which is not only an entertainment but a history and criticism of contemporary morals.[16]

Defining morals as the habits of the majority, Shaw next proceeds to explain the theatrical expectations of the average middle-class playgoer, who soliloquizes:

> If I am to have any sense of security, I must be able to reckon on other people behaving in a certain ascertained way. Never mind whether it is the ideally right way or the ideally wrong way: it will suit me well enough if only it is convenient and, above all, unmistakeable. Lay it down if you like that people are not to pay debts and are to murder one another whenever they get a chance. In that case I can refuse to give credit, and can carry weapons and learn to use them to defend myself. On the other hand, if you settle that debts are to be enforced and the peace kept by the police, I will give credit and renounce the practice of arms. But the one thing that I cannot stand is not knowing what the social contract is.[17]

Finally, as to critics:

> [They have grown so accustomed to plots and formulae] that at last they cannot relish or understand a play that has grown naturally. ... They are like peasants who are so accustomed to

food reeking with garlic that when food is served to them without it they declare that it has no taste at all,[18]

a statement confirmed by Archer's disgruntled declaration after *Widowers' Houses* that Shaw had no specific talents as a dramatist. That it is Archer, not Shaw, who has to be identified for the average middle-class playgoer today is some measure of the continuing success of the principles of Shavian dramaturgy.

NOTES

1 From the Preface to *The Shewing up of Blanco Posnet* in *The Complete Prefaces of Bernard Shaw* (London, 1965), p. 410.
2 *The Collected Letters of Bernard Shaw*, ed. Dan H. Laurence (New York, 1966), p. 176.
3 *Ibid.*, p. 188.
4 Eden Greville, "Bernard Shaw and his Plays," *Munsey's Magazine*, XXXIV (1906), 765–6.
5 From the Preface to *Plays Pleasant and Unpleasant, The Unpleasant Plays* (London, 1952), vol. I, pp. ix–xi.
6 *Letters*, p. 384.
7 John Maddison Morton, *Box and Cox* (New York, Samuel French, n.d.). (First produced at the Olympic Theatre, London, 1847.)
8 *Letters*, p. 222.
9 *Ibid.*, p. 632.
10 *Ibid.*, p. 395.
11 *Ibid.*, p. 345.
12 Preface to *Three Plays by Brieux* (New York, 1911), p. xxiv.
13 *Ibid.*, p. xxv.
14 *Ibid.*, p. xxvi.
15 *Ibid.*, p. xviii.
16 *Ibid.*, p. vii.
17 *Ibid.*, pp. xxxiv–v.
18 *Ibid.*, pp. xxiii–iv.

STANLEY WEINTRAUB

Genesis of a Play: Two Early Approaches to Man and Superman

As much as Bernard Shaw admired *Don Giovanni,* it was becoming clear by the end of the 1880s that he was searching for his personal recasting of Mozart's concept. Although he had already written that *Don Giovanni* "is as superior to Romeo [and Juliet] as a sonnet by Shakespeare to a sonnet by Adelaide Proctor ... ,"[1] he was confessing, a few years later, "Ever since I was a boy I have been in search of a satisfactory performance of Don Giovanni; and I have at last come to see that Mozart's turn will hardly be in my time." The fault, he thought, lay as much in the libretto as in the musical demands upon its performers. "Take a pot of paste, a scissors and some tissue paper," he went on, and began sketching a redramatization of the action.[2] He had, already, unknowingly sketched some tentative workings-out even earlier than his music-critic carping about the great opera's deficiencies; but development of his ideas about the Don into *Man and Superman* and its *Don Juan in Hell* play-within-a-play was still far from his mind, and more than a decade away.

Literarily, Shaw went to hell twice, both times inspired by Mozart's Don, whom he thought "the first Byronic hero in music."[3] (Facets of the Byronic Juan attracted Shaw, especially Byron's irresistibility to, and his pursuit by, the opposite sex, and his ironic inversion of, and sardonic comments upon, conventional values.) A short story written in August 1887 was his first working-out of the legend. The later Shavian Don Juan is an extension of this earlier view of the Don as too puritanical and too spiritual to be satisfied by purely physical amours – a man who spends his time running from amorous women, and whose reputation as a lover is based on the fabrications of his servant and the wish-fulfilment slanders of slighted females.

The 1887 tale[4] is told in the first person by a young woman who had gone to the opera one evening to see *Don Giovanni* – a performance she castigates in the best Corno di Bassetto style.* Afterwards she returns on a suburban train, alone in her compartment – alone, at least, until, while daydreaming about the real Don, she observes him sitting opposite her, in his traditional costume. When he realizes that he has been discovered he asks her to remain calm. "Pray be quiet," he says. "You are alone. I am only what you call a ghost, and have not the slightest interest in meddling with you." At that point the story turns into what seems to be a preliminary scenario for *Don Juan in Hell*, with the Lady an equivalent to the Hell Scene's Dona Ana, who finds herself at the opening of the scene face to face with an equally ethereal Don Juan.

Other than Juan's confession of his first having been seduced by an amorous widow – something which had happened to the writer of the story just two years before, when Mrs. Jenny Pat-

* "The Don was a conceited Frenchman, with a toneless, dark, nasal voice, and such a tremolo that he never held a note steady long enough to let us hear whether it was in tune or not. Leporello was a pudgy, vulgar Italian buffo, who quacked instead of singing. The tenor, a reedy creature, left out Dall sua pace because he couldnt trust himself to get through it. The parts of Masetto and the Commendatore were doubled: I think by the call-boy. As to the women, Donna Anna was fat and fifty; Elvira was a tearing, gasping, 'dramatic' soprano, whose voice I expected to hear break across every time she went higher than F sharp; and Serlina, a beginner on her trial trip, who finished Batti, batti and Vedrai carino with cadenzas out of the mad scene in Lucia, was encored for both in consequence. The orchestra was reinforced by local amateurs, the brass parts being played on things from the band of the 10th Hussars. Everybody was delighted; ..." (Actually Shaw did not begin doing music reviews for *The Star* as "Corno di Bassetto" until a year after the story was written.)

terson initiated him at age 29 into that phase of manhood – the rest of the tale has the ring of the later Shaw. The posthumous relationship of the Don with the father of Ana, the Commander, is similar. "He has since confessed," the Don tells the Lady, "that he was in the wrong; and we are now very good friends; especially as I have never set up any claim to superiority as a swordsman on the strength of our encounter, but have admitted freely that I made a mere lucky thrust in the dark." In the play Juan warns Ana that her father "will be mortally offended if you speak of me as his murderer! He maintains that he was a much better swordsman than I. ... I never dispute the point; so we are excellent friends."

Like his Shavian predecessor (and Shaw himself), the play's Juan finds his first amorous experience the result of being thrown into the arms of a designing female. But where the play requires a background of understanding of the Don Juan myth, the story goes into all the events Mozart celebrated, although deromanticizing them. In the play Shaw is content to have his Don victimized by the man-devouring Life Force, and then attempt his escape from the alluring women in which the Force was incarnated. ("I ran away from it. I ran away from it very often: in fact I became famous for running away from it.")

More curious is the resemblance of the concepts of heaven and hell in the Shavian short story to those in the Hell Scene. The principals of the Hell Scene learn that the frontier of heaven and hell is "only the difference between two ways of looking at things," and Ana is told that they "see each other as bodies only because we learnt to think about one another under that aspect when we were alive." The Don of the story had told the Lady, "If I speak of it [hell] as a place at all, I do so in order to make my narrative comprehensible, just as I express myself to you phenomenally as a gentleman in hat, cloak, and boots, although such things are no part of the category to which I belong." The hell of the play is a place for vulgar satisfaction of the senses, and the devil is the leader of its best society. The Don grudgingly acknowledges the Devil's intellectual and debating gifts, and resents his cordiality. In the story, the Don tells the Lady, "I found society there composed chiefly of the vulgar, hysterical, brutish, weak, good-for-nothing people, all well-intentioned, who kept up the reputation of the place by making themselves and each other as unhappy as they were capable of being. They wearied and disgusted me; and I disconcerted them beyond measure. The Prince of Darkness is not a gentleman. His knowledge and insight are very remarkable as far as they go; but they do not go above the level of his crew. He kept up a certain pretence of liking my company and conversation; and I was polite to him.... Still, I felt that the cordiality of our relations was a strain on us both."

The germ of the "plot" of the Hell Scene – if one is willing to admit that the "Shavio-Socratic" quartet has a plot – also appears in the short story. Juan in the play finds his temperament incompatible with the philosophy by which the dwellers in pleasure-satisfied hell live, and determines to transfer his abode to heaven, where life is dry and austere, and the inhabitants find enjoyment of anything an untrustworthy sensation. The Devil encourages his departure, not wanting Juan's subversive ideas permeating hell. "Not that we don't admire your intellect, you know," says the Devil diplomatically. "We do. But ... you dont get on with us. The place doesnt suit you. Why not take refuge in heaven? That's the proper place for you." He makes it clear that anyone can go if his taste lies that way – that the gulf between heaven and hell is only the difference between the angelic and the diabolic temperament. "Have you ever been," the Devil explains to Ana, "in the country where I have the largest following? England. There they have great racecourses, and also concert rooms where they play ... Mozart. Those who go to the racecourses can stay away from them and go to the classical concerts if they like .... But do the lovers of racing desert their sport and flock to the concert room? Not they. They would suffer there all the weariness the Commander has suffered in heaven."

In almost the same language, the earlier Don had explained his predicament to the lady of the short story. He had been informed while in hell, he said, "that the Prince [of Darkness] had publicly said that my coming to the place was all a mistake, and that he wished I would go to heaven and be blest ... I went at once to the Prince ... He first said, in a coarse conversational style which always grated on me, that my informant was a liar; but on my refusing to accept that explanation he sulkily apologized, and assured me, first, that he had only wished me to go to heaven because he honestly thought – though he could not sympathize with my taste – that I should be more comfortable there; and, second, that my coming into his set was really a mistake." When Juan asks why he was then detained in hell, the Devil reassures him that he can leave whenever he desires, as can anyone of similar tastes. Sceptically, Juan inquires why the dwellers in hell took little advantage of such freedom. "I can only make his reply intelligible to you," Juan tells the Lady, "by saying that the devils do not go for exactly the same reason that your English betting men do not frequent the Monday Popular Concerts, though they are as free to go to them as you are. But the Devil was good enough to say that perhaps heaven would suit me. He warned me that the heavenly people were unfeeling, uppish, precise, and frightfully dry in their conversation and amusements. However, I could try them; and if I did not like them, I could come back."

As lines in the short story of August 1887 are compared with the dialogue of the play written between 1901 and 1903, it becomes more and more clear that the resemblances are too uncanny to be coincidental. If we read backwards from the standpoint of chronology, "Don Giovanni Explains" seems to render in indirect speech many of the lines Shaw gives to characters in *Don Juan in Hell*. However, the creative process must have been exactly the reverse, Shaw expanding the somewhat stilted indirect speech of the unsuccessful fiction into the sharp and eloquent ironies of the play-within-a-play.

In the story, Juan had reported to the Lady that the Devil had warned him that if he "wanted real heart and feeling and sentiment, honest, wholesome robust humor, and harmless love of sport, I should have to come back to them for it. I told him frankly that I did not intend to come back ... His vulgarity jarred every fibre in me; but he was quite honest in it. ..." Now, the play's reworking of the Devil's "amiable" invitation: "Fare you well, Don Juan ... I wish you every happiness: heaven, as I said before, suits some people. But if you should change your mind, do not forget that the gates are always open here to the repentant prodigal. If you feel at any time that warmth of heart, sincere unforced affection, innocent enjoyment, and warm, breathing, palpitating reality – " and at that point Juan interrupts irreverently – as the Prince of Darkness complains – "to throw my friendly farewell back in my teeth ... ." Since the Don of the story could hardly have overheard the Devil's gloomy complaint afterward, that Juan's departure was "a political defeat," the lines that follow in the dramatic adaptation belong only to the play.

Although one scholar of the Don Juan myth has insisted that Shaw's philosophical romp "has really nothing of the Tenorio legend *in its action,*"[5] the relationship of the early short story to the play shows more than the accident of inception. The ties of *Man and Superman* – minus its Hell Scene – to the legend of the irresistible and apparently heartless Don are more tenuous, but Shaw does have characters from the contemporary (and major) portion of the play enact their mythic counterparts in the Hell Scene. Ann, Octavius, and John Tanner have their obvious parallels, and Tanner (who even claims descent from Don Juan Tenorio) has his Leporello in his chauffeur 'Enry Straker. Ramsden, Ann's father-surrogate, is the Commander; and Mendoza, the talkative and ineffectual brigand-chieftain in the Sierras, is a comic grotesque of the Devil. Still, however much John Tanner might have claimed his ancestry from the Don, his Shavian ancestry is somewhat mixed, for he also sounds and acts a good deal like the hero of the last completed Shaw novel, Sidney Trefusis.

Shaw began his fifth novel, *An Unsocial Socialist*, when he was twenty-seven, in July 1883. (Its working title was *The Heartless Man.*) Having recently become converted to the faith, it was almost inevitable that Shaw would draw the hero of his novel – like the later Tanner – as a Marxian socialist. Born a capitalist because of inherited wealth, he uses his tainted income ("Every halfpenny I possess is stolen money; but it has been stolen legally and I have no means of restoring it to the rightful owners even if I felt inclined to") in quixotic efforts to destroy capitalism. The first part of the novel is half early-socialist realism, half *opera bouffé*, whereas the second seems an early working-out of many of the elements of *Man and Superman*. A critic, prefacing a reprint of the novel, concluded that the "high-comedic style" was reminiscent of the Shavian plays: "A periphery of deliberate perversity contains the core of deep seriousness. The hero, Trefusis, is an analogue of Tanner in *Man and Superman*."[6] Nevertheless, Sidney Trefusis is more than an analogue to Tanner; his characteristics seem a working-out of the personality Shaw did not yet know he would develop more memorably as John Tanner. Not only are both impudent and zealous young Marxists, but both spend their large unearned incomes guiltily in the production and distribution of socialist publications. Trefusis also writes and edits a socialist journal; and, he adds, "I occupy myself partly in working out a scheme for the reorganization of industry, and partly in attacking my own class, women and all ... ." Tanner even appends to his name as author of *The Revolutionist's Handbook*, which he has published at his own expense, the letters "M.I.R.C." – Member of the Idle Rich Class. And he is equally devoted to the extinction of his class.

Chichester Erskine, the dapper but mediocre poet whose romantic appeal to women is as ineffectual as his verse, is the Octavius of the novel. Although Shaw in his Preface to the play claimed (very likely sincerely) that he took the character over unaltered from Mozart's Ottavio, there are strong and possibly unconscious resemblances to the elegant Erskine. "I want to count for something as a poet," Octavius confesses: "I want to write a great play." Erskine has already written his first play, a turgid poetic tragedy entitled *The Patriot Martyrs*; and although it had not been performed, he was already, according to Shaw, "bent on writing another drama, without regard to the exigencies of the stage; but he had not begun it .... ." Still, he had a title – after the name of the imperious young woman with whom he had fallen hopelessly in love.

Octavius is even more hopelessly smitten, but his beloved has already set herself to the capture of Tanner. Both Tanner and Trefusis, in fact, "are hunted by desperately biological females."* Tanner's Ann Whitefield and Trefusis's Agatha Wylie are both fatherless, wards of men with whom their intended prey have business and social contacts; and both young women are irreverent, strong, and sly, able to get their way with their elders. (They even have the same initials.) Their victims-to-be are both set against marriage. "Men should marry, especially rich men," Trefusis confesses. "But I assure you I have no present intention of doing so." Later he tells Agatha, "I could not refuse a woman anything she had set her heart upon – except my hand in marriage. As long as your sex are content to stop short of that, they can do as they please with me."

It is the beginning of a "duel of sex" which, when refashioned† by a more experienced hand for the last act of *Man and Superman*, was considered the ironic and witty peer of the Mirabell-Millamant courtship scene in Congreve's *The Way of the World*. (Nothing like it had appeared on the English stage

* William Irvine, "Bernard Shaw's Early Novels," *Trollopian* II (1947), 41–2. The huntress figure in *An Unsocial Socialist* is the unswervingly passionate first wife of Trefusis, Henrietta, whom Shaw kills off in the first part of the novel. His Ann Whitefield possesses traits which seem an amalgam of Henrietta and Agatha.

† The similarities to the novel suggest that this was not an unconscious borrowing.

for two hundred years.) "How cruel!" Agatha had sarcastically answered Trefusis for waving aside the idea that he ought to marry.

"Do take pity on our poor sex," said Agatha maliciously. "You are so rich, and so very clever, and really so nice-looking that you ought to share yourself with somebody ... ."

Trefusis grinned and shook his head, slowly but emphatically.

"I suppose *I* should have no chance," continued Agatha pathetically.

"I should be delighted, of course," he replied with simulated confusion, but with a lurking gleam in his eye that might have checked her, had she noticed it.

"Do marry me, Mr. Trefusis," she pleaded, clasping her hands in a rapture of mischievous raillery. "Pray do."

"Thank you," said Trefusis determinedly; "I will."

"I am very sure you shant," said Agatha, after an incredulous pause, springing up and gathering her skirt as if to run away. "You do not suppose I was in earnest, do you?"

"Undoubtedly I do. *I* am in earnest."

Agatha hesitated, uncertain whether he might not be playing with her as she had just been playing with him. "Take care," she said. "I may change my mind and be in earnest too; and then how will you feel, Mr. Trefusis?"

"I think, under our altered relations, you had better call me Sidney."

"I think we had better drop the joke. It was in rather bad taste; and I should not have made it, perhaps."

"It would be an execrable joke: therefore I have no intention of regarding it as one. You shall be held to your offer, Agatha. Are you in love with me?"

"Not in the least. Not the very smallest bit in the world. I do not know anybody with whom I am less in love or less likely to be in love."

"Then you must marry me. If you were in love with me, I should run away ... ."

"You should never have a chance of running away from me."

"I shall not want to. I am not so squeamish as I was ... ."

"But I was only joking: I don't care for you ... ."

"Agatha," he said with grim patience: "half an hour ago I had no more intention of marrying you than of making a voyage to the moon. But when you made the suggestion, I felt all its force in an instant; and now nothing will satisfy me but your keeping your word. Of all the women I know, you are the only one not quite a fool."

"I should be a great fool if –"

"If you married me, you were going to say; but I don't think so. I am the only man, not quite an ass, of your acquaintance. I know my value, and yours."*

Soon the marriage is planned for "before the end of next month," as Trefusis contemplates attending a socialist conference in Geneva – the perfect honeymoon for an unsentimental Shavian heroine and an unsuccessfully unsocial socialist.

The Tanner-Ann Whitefield proposal scene begins and ends in the same way, as Ann tells Tanner, "You ought to get married." Tanner explodes with a series of "I wont marry you" outbursts, and Ann answers placidly that no one has asked him to, adding eventually, "Well, if you dont want to be married, you needn't be." Again the variations on the theme concern the possibility of Tanner's running away, the fact that they do not love each other, and the denials that each is out to fascinate the other into submission. Soon the jests turn to earnest, each *no* of Tanner's getting stronger in noise content and weaker in real force. But when Ann admits that he *has* said *no* – that she has made a mistake after all – Tanner confesses that he is, in spite of himself, in the grip of the same force† that enchanted Trefusis. "I solemnly say that I am not a happy man," he announces when the betrothal becomes public; yet like Trefusis he intends to get married quickly – and continue his proselytizing. The wedding gifts, Tanner vows, "will be instantly sold, and the proceeds devoted to circulating free copies of *The Revolutionist's Handbook*."

With the greater dialogue opportunities of the play form, and with love affairs, marriage, play criticism, and playwriting be-

* The text of quotations from *An Unsocial Socialist* follows the first edition (1887).

† Tanner actually labels it the "Life Force." To Trefusis it is only a "force."

hind him, Shaw – juxtaposing the unlikely ingredients of high comedy of manners and anthropological myth – could produce expansively, in the first years of the twentieth century, one of the century's great plays. In spite of all that had happened to him, and all he had accomplished himself in that fertile period, the "socialist" novel and the Juanesque short story of the futile mid-eighties had reached across the years to help determine what form *Man and Superman* would take.

NOTES

1 Bernard Shaw as "Corno di Bassetto," music review dated 17 July 1889, reprinted from *The Star* (London) in *London Music in* 1888–89 (London, 1937), p. 142.
2 Bernard Shaw, music review dated 13 May 1891, reprinted from *The World* (London) in *Music in London* 1890–94 (London, 1932), I, 187.
3 Bernard Shaw as "Corno di Bassetto," music review dated 7 August 1889, reprinted from *The Star* (London) in *London Music*, I, 190.
4 Bernard Shaw, "Don Giovanni Explains," in *The Black Girl in Search of God and Some Lesser Tales* (London, 1934), pp. 169–90. (Dated 1 August 1887.)
5 Oscar Mandel, *The Theatre of Don Juan* (Lincoln, Nebraska, 1963), p. 548.
6 Arthur Zeiger, Preface to *Selected Novels of Bernard Shaw* (New York, 1946), p. x.

R. B. PARKER

The Circle *of Somerset Maugham*

Superficially, there are enough resemblances between Bernard Shaw and Somerset Maugham to justify the inclusion of *The Circle* in the repertory of the Shaw Festival at Niagara-on-the-Lake this summer. They were contemporaries, each celebrated for comedies revealing attitudes toward sex and money that shocked their more conventional audiences and made them the two most popular English dramatists of the first half of the twentieth century. But it requires only the experience of seeing their work together to be reminded of how very different they really are. And, though the contrast is largely in Shaw's favour, it also helps to clarify the qualities that are peculiarly Maugham's and casts light on the reasons for his narrower achievement.

Considered in terms of their basic philosophies and modes of life and of their particular dramatic techniques, one can hardly think of two writers with less in common: Shaw the ascetic vegetarian in eccentric homespuns, the socialist who looked on art as propaganda and wrote comedies of ideas; Maugham the sybarite and dandy, darling of the salons and the Riviera smart set, the political cynic who said that he wrote only to entertain. There does not seem to be any record of their ever having met – though surely they must have, in that tight little London literary world at the beginning of the century; nor did Shaw make public his opinion of Somerset Maugham. But Maugham mentions Shaw several times in his literary autobiography *The Summing Up* and in the prefaces to the three volumes of his *Collected Plays*. He always speaks of him with great respect, for Shaw made even more money with plays than Maugham himself did. But there is also apparent a feeling of scarcely veiled exasperation.

The trouble with Shaw was that his stupendous box office success made nonsense of Maugham's formula for "popular" drama and thus, indirectly, of Maugham's justification for the limitations of his plays. Maugham constantly insists[1] that his plays should not be examined too closely by analytical critics: they are for acting, not dissection in the study; he wrote them to make money; his intention was only to entertain: not to instruct but to please. And, believing that the mental common denominator of an audience will always be lower than that of any one of its members, he argues that the way to please an audience is to stir up its emotions, particularly its laughter, but never to presume to try to make it think. "[Comedy] is not a work of edification," he says, "... and if it castigates the follies of the moment that is by the way and only in so far as this no doubt laudable process occasions laughter. The object is the entertainment of the audience, not their improvement."[2] "I have a notion that when the intelligent look for thought in a playhouse, they show less intelligence than one would have expected of them."[3]

This argument may explain certain characteristics of Maugham's own plays, but as a generalization about prose comedy it obviously founders on the popularity of Shaw's comedy of ideas. And it is amusing, but saddening, to see how Maugham twists in an effort to avoid this contradiction. Shaw's ideas were not really *original*, he hazards, but merely the common culture of his day; Shaw was popular because he pandered to the English audiences' fascinated distrust of sexual passion (a comment, incidentally, which might be applied to Maugham's own work);

finally, he is forced back to the weak distinction that Shaw succeeded "not because he is a dramatist of ideas but because he is a dramatist. But he is inimitable."[4]

There is a similar fuzziness in his comments on dramatic prose. At one point we find him arguing that prose can have "dramatic" interest only if it reflects the minutiae of contemporary slang and that this necessarily makes prose drama as evanescent as yesterday's newspaper;[5] but elsewhere we find him *attacking* the notion that dramatic prose should report speech "realistically" because this so often fails to convey profundities of meaning.[6] These contradictions do not invalidate Maugham's critical writings, of course, which remain a most interesting insight into the mind of a serious artist. But they do suggest that Maugham's own comments on his plays should not be treated as the last word on them. There is no need to feel guilty about looking for a serious point of view in them because Maugham warned us from doing so. His attitude toward playwriting was inconsistent; it changed perceptibly during his career, and his claim to have written only to please the public does not explain its vagaries. It is not insignificant, surely, that he began and ended his theatre career by writing serious, questioning plays, which he knew would not be "popular," and that he dropped the theatre eventually because he was "tired of giving half a truth because that was all [the audience] were prepared to take."[7] His cynicism about playwriting, like his cynicism about life in general, must be recognized as at least partly defensive, an attempt to protect vulnerable uncertainties by pretending never to have had any very ambitious aims.

Specifically, it should be recognized that there is a serious level to *The Circle*.* Despite a surface hardness, which drew catcalls from the gallery on its first night and led to its being banned in the U.S.S.R. as recently as 1946, *The Circle* is by no means a cynical play. In fact, cynicism – the stereotyped view of

* John Gielgud's successful 1944 revival of *The Circle* stressed this serious aspect of the play.

Maugham himself – is included and devalued within the play itself in the person of Clive Champion-Cheney. Rather *The Circle* is a problem play about the relationship between individual instinct and society, and it reveals an unresolved contradiction of attitude, which was presumably Maugham's own. It combines a mixture of romanticism and cynicism that was ideally suited to the bitter-sweet mood of the 1920s, the age of Noel Coward and Scott Fitzgerald, so that Alec Waugh can talk of Maugham as a "mouthpiece for the decade."[8] And this ambiguity occurs throughout Maugham's work, whether we see it with H. E. Bates as mere "tin-foil cynicism" wrapped around sentimentality and a basic fear of emotion,[9] or more kindly with R. H. Ward as "laughter held in bondage to grief ... a kind of defence against 'the callousness of the universe.' "[10]

Let us consider first the social implications of the play. Along with *Our Betters, The Unattainable, Home and Beauty,* and *The Constant Wife, The Circle* belongs to Maugham's second spurt of play-writing, just after the First World War. Maugham places this group of plays in the tradition of the comedy of manners:

> They are written in the tradition which flourished so brightly in the Restoration Period, which was carried on by Goldsmith and Sheridan, and which, since it has had so long a vogue, may be supposed to have something in it that peculiarly appeals to the English temper. The people who do not like it describe it as artificial comedy and by that epithet foolishly think they condemn it. It is drama not of action, but of conversation. It treats with indulgent cynicism the humours, follies and vices of the world of fashion. It is urbane, sentimental at times, for that is the English character, and a trifle unreal. It does not preach: sometimes it draws a moral, but with a shrug of the shoulders as if to invite you to lay no too great stress on it.[11]

The tradition is further defined by N. W. Sawyer in his book *The Comedy of Manners from Sheridan to Maugham.* It is a comedy, he says, for

> reflecting the life, thought, and manners of upperclass society,

> faithful to its traditions and philosophy. It is intellectually and dispassionately conceived, in the nature of a detached commentary, in which the only moral considerations are sincerity and fidelity to the facts of the society represented. The attitude of the playwright is, at least theoretically, unpartisan, although it is difficult for a latent flavour of satire to be kept out entirely. Characters may emerge into complete individuality, but more often universal traits give way to those types into which the world of fashion inclines to reproduce itself. Dialogue is naturally of more than ordinary importance, for the leisure of this world promotes the cultivation of verbal smartness, and this smartness dialogue must display, even if at the expense of naturalness. And, lastly, one feels a certain idealization of the whole picture – a heightening of values, a seasoning of effects, an acceleration of tempo.[12]

Comedy of manners, then, is a form that reflects the surface pattern that an exclusive social minority has imposed upon the disorderly realities of life – particularly on the sex instinct – and that finds its essence in substituting witty conversation for dangerous actions. It is partly "realistic" in that it reflects actual manners, but it is far more brilliantly consistent than anything in real life; and this gives it an element of exaggeration which may be turned satirically on itself. Thus our pleasure in the form is double-edged: we delight in the wit and skill of the manners themselves and laugh at characters too inept to play the game, but we also delight in the way that the system fails, when instinct insists on breaking out despite the exaggerated controls.

These complexities are easily seen in *The Circle*. The realistic aspect of its setting, manners, and conversation needs no emphasis – indeed, in the case of Teddy Luton, it can be argued that realistic colloquialism is overdone; but for all this, the play is quite obviously artificial, a clever literary construction. The conversation is consistently wittier than we can hope for in real life, though, to Maugham's credit, it almost always seems to arise from the characters and situation. Most of the epigrams in the play come from Clive Champion-Cheney, his "There is no more lamentable pursuit than a life of pleasure," for example, or "I suppose it's difficult for the young to realise that one may be old without being a fool," or "A woman will always sacrifice herself if you give her the opportunity. It is her favourite form of self-indulgence." Champion-Cheney is far more self-consciously "mannered" than the other speakers, so it is appropriate for him to speak epigrams; but most of the play's wit arises more directly from the situation and cannot be anthologized. For example, we need to know that Champion-Cheney is the injured husband and Hugh Porteus the disillusioned seducer to appreciate the wit of the following:

> *C.-C.* My dear Hughie, you were my greatest friend. I trusted you. It may have been rash.
> *Porteus* It was inexcusable.

And if we did not know that he had been cuckolded, we should miss the irony of Champion-Cheney's reply when Elizabeth says that she imagines Kitty must now be slight and frail, "Frail, certainly." The only false note in the wit comes with Elizabeth herself, because Maugham seems not to have decided how much she belongs to the world of manners, whether she is to be considered an ingenue or a witty lady. Her early interchange with Champion-Cheney seems laboured:

> *C.-C.* I'm never cross with a woman under thirty.
> *Eliz.* Oh, then I've got ten years.
> *C.-C.* Mathematics?
> *Eliz.* No. Paint.

And her epigram, "I don't think you want too much sincerity in society. It would be like an iron girder in a house of cards," stands out awkwardly from the surrounding text, too striking for the speaker or the situation. On the whole, though, the wit is splendid.

The action, too, is patterned with a care that removes it from reality. It obeys all three of the so-called "dramatic unities." It has one location: the drawing-room of Champion-Cheney's country house. Its timespan is limited to about eight hours, from midmorning to just after dinner on the same day. It has a single action, which is easily summarized in the infinitive form advocated by Stanislavski as "Elizabeth to repeat her mother-in-law's elopement." And, as usual in Maugham, it all grows out of a single clever situation[13] – the idea that Elizabeth arranges a visit of the older lovers in order to clarify her own feelings for Teddy Luton and her boredom with her husband.

Our attitude toward the elopement is switchbacked from an initial recognition of its attractiveness, through a revulsion from its dangers, to a final acceptance of its deeper necessity and value. The whole structure is very clever and *The Circle* deserves its reputation as Maugham's best play. Maugham himself, however, had one reservation about it, which scarcely seems justified: "I have always thought that the device suggested by Clive Champion-Cheney to his son to prevent Elizabeth running away not very happy. I should have liked at that point a more substantial and dramatic invention."[14] The very literariness of the device of blackmailing by generosity, however (a cynical misapplication of Ibsen's psychology in *The Lady from the Sea*), is surely quite appropriate to Clive Champion-Cheney, who is an overclever intellectual; and its hypocrisy has the useful effect of alienating whatever sympathy the audience may have left for the abandoned father and son.

One implication of the title, then, is the sense of circular structure, the younger generation repeating its elders' past behaviour. Another implication, less obvious but no less important, is that this repetition is the result of living in a particular "social *circle*," an exclusive group whose nature provokes this sort of reaction. The milieu in question is, of course, the typical manners circle of wealthy leisure, where the rituals of upperclass social life have become the main standards by which to judge a man. The artificiality of this way of life is nicely caught by the play's emphasis on furniture, clothes, photographs, and, especially, bridge playing.

Arnold's fussy affectation is neatly established at the start by his concern for the exact placing of his furniture, and his incompetence even at manners is revealed when he is unable to decide if his new chair is really antique, when challenged by Lord Porteus. He has to run to find a picture of it to be sure. His "passion," he says, is for decorating houses; "a man marries to have a home, but also because he doesn't want to be bothered with sex and all that sort of thing." (Not unnaturally, Elizabeth objects that "These over-decorated houses are like a prison in which I can't breathe.") In contrast, Arnold's father, Clive Champion-Cheney, is almost perfectly Restoration in his ability to manipulate manners so as to indulge his antisocial instincts. The play does not have a villain, but if it had, he would be it. Even before he gloats to Kitty about his succession of young mistresses, his cynicism is apparent. When asked what sort of person Lord Porteus was, he replies that he wore his clothes better than any man in London and had a very good figure: manners praise which is scarcely flattering about a man who was considered for prime minister. His meeting with Teddy is typical:

C.-C. How do you do? Do you play bridge?
Luton I do.
C.-C. Capital. Do you declare without top honours?
Luton Never.
C.-C. Of such is the kingdom of heaven. I see that you are a good young man.

Bridge is an appropriate symbol of upperclass manners, since not only is it a favourite occupation in that "house of cards," but its sense of ritualized competition reflects the manoeuvrings for personal advantage beneath the surface of fine manners. Maugham employs it in *Our Betters* to reveal the tension between manners and explosive sexual jealousy; and here in *The Circle* he uses it to expose the exasperated relationship between Porteus and Lady Kitty and the way that Champion-Cheney can use the rules maliciously to torment his old rival. This malicious misuse of manners appears even more clearly when Champion-Cheney politely produces the album of photographs to remind Kitty of the ideal of social grace and beauty from which she has fallen.

But is is here that Champion-Cheney loses the audience's sympathy. To this point we have been kept carefully on his side. He has been amiable and witty – though perhaps suspiciously polysyllabic, a little self-indulgently pedantic. Kitty and Porteus, on the other hand, have revealed themselves as ludicrous. We have been encouraged to laugh at them as bad players of the manners game. Kitty affects what J. C. Trewin calls a "tweeting sweeting"[15] image of a scatterbrained young girl, although she is fifty-seven, and the incongruity of this is emphasized by her clothes and absurdly unnatural red hair. Porteus is eccentric in clothes and explosive in temper, and his absurdity is pointed by giving him loose dentures. One of the funniest lines of the play, arising completely from situation and character yet pure comedy of manners in its implications, is Champion-Cheney's reply to Elizabeth when she reminds him that he too has false teeth: "Yes, but damn it all, they fit."

Champion-Cheney emphasizes that these lapses of Lord Porteus and Kitty are the result of their having to live in the vulgar demimonde, to move, as it were, in vicious circles, when respectable society has rejected them: "We are the creatures of our environment. She's a silly, worthless woman because she's led a silly, worthless life." And both Lady Kitty and Lord Porteus seem to agree with him: "because we couldn't get the society we'd been used to we became used to the society we could get," says Kitty, and Porteus warns Elizabeth: "Man is a gregarious animal. We're members of a herd. If we break the herd's laws we suffer for it. And we suffer damnably."

But when Champion-Cheney reduces Kitty to tears by introducing a photograph of the loveliness she has lost, our assessment of the situation is suddenly and with dazzling skill reversed. Not only do we react with Elizabeth against Champion-Cheney's malice and pity Lady Kitty (since, after all, aging is not a degeneration one is personally responsible for), but there is also an unexpected warmth and tenderness suddenly revealed between the two old lovers. It is only briefly touched on, and the manners surface is quickly re-established by having them begin to flatter one another comically and return to their absurd argument about the viceroyship of India; but the moment has been enough. Warm human feeling has been set up as a rival value to the urbane but complacently self-centered rationalism of Champion-Cheney.

This, and not the decision of the two young lovers, is the heart of the play. The key question is less whether Elizabeth will elope than whether Lady Kitty would do so if she had her chance again. In spite of the misery which resulted, was there not a sufficient justification in the lovers' passion at the time? Elizabeth compares its quality (a little tritely) to the beauty of a flower:

> This morning I happened to notice a rose in the garden. It was all overblown and bedraggled. It looked like a painted old woman. And I remembered that I looked at it a day or two ago. It was lovely then, fresh and blooming and fragrant. It may be hideous, now, but that doesn't take away from the beauty it had once. That was real.

She sets a natural image, the rose, against the static ideal of the photograph album; instinct is balanced against manners. The result appears to be a draw. The play ends with Champion-Cheney laughing at the supposedly thwarted lovers and Kitty and Hugh Porteus laughing at him. None of them has learned by experience; each has repeated his former pattern of behaviour. This is the true "circle" of the play. And the ambiguous attitude toward sexual passion with which it leaves one is typical of Maugham. Like the hero of his most famous novel, he seems to have felt that passion makes life vivid and intense but that it is socially and psychologically destructive, a "human bondage."

This repeated circle and careful balance of *pro* and *con* is obscured, however, by the elopement of Elizabeth and Teddy Luton. Superficially, of course, this is the most obvious circle, a repetition of the earlier choice. But actually it is not a true circle. When examined, the values that motivate Elizabeth and Teddy are found to be different from those that moved Kitty and Lord Porteus. A third alternative to the society-instinct struggle is suggested, which blurs the focus by denying the whole manners assumption on which the play is built.

Consider Elizabeth. At first glance her position seems very like Lady Kitty's, thirty years before. She is 25, Lady Kitty was 27. The resemblance of Arnold and his father is stressed, though obviously Arnold is even more inhibited than Clive: he regards his wife merely as a valuable possession, gratifying to exhibit at dinner parties. Elizabeth is strongly attracted to Teddy Luton who opposes a passion for natural beauty against Arnold's aestheticism; she romanticizes the earlier elopement, therefore; and, even when the appearance of Kitty and Porteus has disillusioned her, she insists that what was once beautiful was its own justification. However, despite these sympathies between Elizabeth and Kitty, there are also obvious and crucial differences. Elizabeth is not a featherbrain and she is going into the affair with her eyes wide open to its dangers. She is not abandoning a child, and the life she is to expect is clearly differentiated from the one that Kitty and Lord Porteus have led.

This of course derives from the great difference between Porteus and Teddy Luton. Teddy is a colonial, an outsider in the manners society. With unconscious irony he is described by Arnold as a "bull in a china shop," and he comments about himself, "I've often thought I wasn't quite a gentleman." England seems to him "full of people doing things they don't want to because other people expect it of them." His difference from the others is not due to class, however, but to money, or rather to the lack of it. Arnold sneers that "He hasn't got a bob." This insistence on the exclusive money basis of contemporary mores is typical of Maugham, and distinguishes him from the earlier writers of comedy of manners, even from his immediate predecessor, Oscar Wilde. Teddy's inability to fit into a manners framework is comically illustrated in his wooing of Elizabeth. With a phrasing reminiscent of Wilde's insistence on the importance of treating serious things frivolously, Teddy protests that love is "all so serious and I think we ought to keep emotion out of it." However, he is incapable of sublimating his feelings in this way, and his passion takes the form first of irritation with Elizabeth and then of an outright declaration, which sweeps her off her feet.

Teddy belongs to a romantic, rather Kiplingesque tendency in Maugham to idealize colonialism. (Bessie Saunders, the Jamesian heroine of *Our Betters*, is another example.) He wins Elizabeth because he offers her, not the exiled luxury that ruined Kitty, but a life of meaningful effort in the Malay States, where happiness depends not on social institutions but on individual strength of character: "... if they're empty headed [says Teddy], then they're just faced with their own emptiness and they're done." And this idea that the choice is not just between stifling conformity and glorious but destructive passion, that for the strong-minded there is a third alternative of recreating their own values, is reiterated approvingly by Porteus at the end when he says to Kitty:

> If we made rather a hash of things perhaps it was because we were rather trivial people. You can do anything in this world if you're prepared to take the consequences, and consequences depend on character.

So *The Circle* ends with the implication that Elizabeth and Teddy will not suffer. Neither Champion-Cheney's urbane conformity nor the flash-in-the-pan of Kitty and Lord Porteus is the right behaviour. They end the play mocking each other, and the audience laughs at both. The true way is to reject the manners context altogether and strongmindedly be true to oneself.

This complete fracturing of the manners framework is an established variant in the comedy of manners tradition: we get a similar effect in Wycherley's *The Plain Dealer*. But, as dealt with in *The Circle*, it is a little unconvincing. There will be different opinions about this, of course, but to the present writer the colonial solution here seems a sentimental oversimplification,

Moreover, the play does not end with the escape. The final mood is more ambiguous, more characteristic of Maugham.

Colonialism partly fails to convince because Teddy Luton is the least satisfactory of the characters. The role seems to be built up mainly by the use of the slang of the 1920s, but as the slang is now archaic – ripping, jolly, beastly, blighter, I say, By Jove, frip, footling, and all that sort of thing – the result is caricature. This may be an accidental result of Maugham's theories about the contemporaneity of dramatic prose, but one suspects that Maugham – or at least half of Maugham – really does consider Teddy an ass; just as his occasional romanticism about colonials is more than balanced by the scathing pictures that he draws of such people in many of his short stories and the ironies of his Canadian play, *The Promised Land*.

One is left then with a final problem. Why is the colonial alternative to the manners opposition of conformity and instinct disappointing? Is it because Maugham was here settling for the half-truth as a box-office sop, offering a sentimental happy ending to soften the unpleasant alternatives of his real vision? Or does it reflect a divided loyalty in Maugham himself? We cannot know, of course. The hard-bitten professionalism of his opinions in *The Summing Up* would lead one to suspect the box-office half-truth, but considering the question in the context of Maugham's writings and life as a whole, it is perhaps fairer to plump for the second. Maugham's whole career seems to have been a struggle between his determination to make a comfortable life for himself by understanding and manipulating the way of the world, his existentialist belief that in a meaningless universe a man has to will his own pattern of values, and his continual nostalgia for a more relaxed trust in the natural rhythms of life – reflected in the final wish-fulfilment marriage of Philip Carey in *Of Human Bondage* or Maugham's own flirtation with the mystic religions of the East. The three alternative values of *The Circle* are constant throughout his work, in fact, and the confused relationship between them must reflect a deep indecision of his own. His attitude toward this confusion fluctuates. At the age of twenty-six he wrote in his *Notebook* that the only possible attitude toward life is one of humorous resignation, but his more characteristic tone is sharper, more negative than that. It seems at the same time detached and unresigned, bitter at its detachment, disdainful of its own mockery, but seeing no alternative. And it is on this characteristic note that *The Circle* finally closes.

Although he insists that communal emotion is the basic ingredient of drama, Maugham says of himself in *The Summing Up*: "I never feel more aloof than when I am in the midst of a throng surrendered to a violent feeling of mirth or sorrow" (p. 54). He stands aloof from the emotions he professionally induces, and in drama the result is irony at the expense of the audience. Thus there is a disturbing mechanicalness about the device of laughter with which he covers the conclusion of *The Circle*. Mirth on stage provokes mirth off stage, of course, as in the laughing gags of the music hall; but as the audience joins in, it cannot be quite sure that it is not laughing at itself. The mockery tends to ramify: we laugh with Champion-Cheney at the idiocy of lovers, with Kitty and Hugh Porteus at the idiocy of restraints. Each thinks that he alone has seen the real joke, including the audience; but each is only partly right. The joke is also on him; the laughter is at his expense too. In the general mirth all standards cancel out. To play on the title for one last time, the circle is now reduced to zero, and, unless the curtain is carefully timed, the situation becomes as uncomfortable as the end of Brook's *Marat-Sade*, where madmen applaud the audience. Maugham tricks us into mirth, then lets us sense an emptiness beneath it.

This amusing but unpleasant effect is characteristically Maugham's own. There is a grittiness of the spirit about his comedy, very different from the life-enhancing exuberance of Shaw. As Maugham says himself in his pamphlet *The Writer's*

Point of View: "When you come down to brass tacks, the value of a work of art depends on the artist's personality" (p. 19). That is the ultimate circle which contains the play.

NOTES

1 Maugham's critical opinions about drama and theatre can be found in *The Summing Up* (Garden City, N.Y., 1938), sections 30–42; *A Writer's Notebook* (London, 1949); *The Writer's Point of View* (London, 1951); the prefaces to the three volumes of his *Collected Plays* (London, 1952); and section 48 of *On a Chinese Screen* (London, 1922). See also his novel *Theatre* (Garden City, NY., 1937) and his final comments on his career in "Looking Back," *Show* (June, July, August 1962).

2 *Collected Plays*, II: ix.

3 *The Summing Up*, p. 131.

4 *Ibid.*, p. 138.

5 *Collected Plays*, I: xviii; *The Summing Up*, p. 122.

6 *Collected Plays*, III: xxiii; *The Summing Up*, p. 141.

7 *The Summing Up*, p. 154.

8 Quoted by John Montgomery, *The Twenties* (London, 1957), p. 210.

9 H. E. Bates, *The Modern Short Story* (London, 1941), p. 145.

10 R. H. Ward, *William Somerset Maugham* (London, 1937), p. 149.

11 *The Summing Up*, p. 121.

12 N. W. Sawyer, *The Comedy of Manners from Sheridan to Maugham* (Philadelphia, 1931), pp. 3–4.

13 For his emphasis on a clever basic "situation," which relates Maugham to the school of Scribe and Sardou, see *Collected Plays*, III: xxi.

14 *Ibid.*, II: xix.

15 See his introductory "Appreciation" in Mander and Mitcheson, *Theatre Companion to Maugham* (London, 1955), p. 7.

WARREN SYLVESTER SMITH

Bernard Shaw and the London Heretics

The decades following 1870 in London were the great years of advocacy for social, political, and religious reform. New guilds, societies, and fellowships appeared monthly, each with its own weekly or monthly journal, each with a set of widely proclaimed principles and aims. The titles ranged alphabetically from "Anti-Aggression" to "Zetetical," and included such causes as free-thought, Christian socialism, co-operation, humanitarianism, a labour church, land reform, population control, Comtist Positivism, and the friends of Russia.

In these same decades the diffident young Dubliner, George B. Shaw, went through the crucible of London art galleries, music halls, theatres, lecture halls, editorial rooms, libraries, committee rooms, outdoor meetings, and ladies' boudoirs to emerge as the delicately adjusted schizophrenic prophet-jokester, Bernard Shaw–GBS. The stormy gatherings of London's heretical societies were the practicum of his belated education. They were, for the most part, his night school. He spent most of his days in the Reading Room of the British Museum. A more effective curriculum can hardly be imagined.

The proliferation of secular-religious heretical societies was made to order for him for two reasons. First, he desperately needed forums in which to develop his skills as a speaker and a committee man. Second, he needed to resolve his own deeply motivated concerns about religion and society. In 1909, in what

* Adapted from *The London Heretics, 1870–1914*, by permission of Constable Publishers, London.

is still the most perceptive all-round critical work on Shaw, G. K. Chesterton made an illuminating observation about him as a prophet: The more ancient variety, Jesus or Socrates, for example, knew what they wanted to say before they said it. For Shaw the act of communication *was* the thought process itself. Shaw could store up information from the British Museum, store up images from galleries and concerts and the view from Dalkey Hill. Before he could make them into a proper pattern for himself, he needed, so to speak, to "try them on," to rub them against other people, to stimulate and to respond, to discard and retain.

When he first came to London at the age of twenty in 1876 to join his mother and his surviving sister, Lucy, he spent a good deal of his time writings novels. He wrote five of them in seven years with hardly any success at all. In the meantime he began to search out the lecture halls, and the story of his finding Henry George and Sidney Webb and finally the Fabians, is so well known it will hardly need attention here. The truth is he joined all sorts of societies. They were often, but not always, committed to a program and a point of view. The London Dialectical Society had been founded in the late sixties to discuss the radical works of John Stuart Mill, but did not normally take sides. Its junior replica, the Zetetical ("truth-seeking") Society began in 1878 with the intent of furnishing "opportunities for the unrestricted discussion of Social, Political, and Philosophical subjects." At either of these, advanced souls were privileged to participate in open consideration of matters generally considered taboo in Victorian drawing rooms. Dr. C. R. Drysdale held forth on "Malthusianism" – the current euphemism for birth control. The practice of cremation received its first impetus from the dialecticals. "The tone was strongly individualistic, atheistic, Malthusian, evolutionary, Ingersollian, Darwinian, Herbert Spencerian," wrote Bernard Shaw, who belonged to both in the days when he was practising public speaking.[1] The tone was also markedly feminist. The dapper Reverend Charles Maurice

Davies, who set himself the obviously enjoyable journalistic task of visiting all the "heterodox" societies in London, found himself in the midst of the dialecticals' discussion of "Chastity." "It was then quite a new sensation for me," he confessed, "to hear ladies discuss those hitherto proscribed subjects, and they were not elderly *bas bleus* either, but young ladies, married and unmarried."[2]

In addition to the Dialectical and Zetetical, Shaw was taken with the literary societies of F. J. Furnivall: the New Shakespeare Society, the Browning Society, the Shelley Society. He mentions also the Bedford Debating Society of Stopford Brooke at Bedford Chapel.[3]

So Shaw became a joiner, but he was careful not to align himself with any organization that committed him to a religious or political point of view to which he could not wholeheartedly subscribe. It was in the end only the Fabian Society that earned his devotion over the years. But he asked questions or made replies wherever he went, and was inevitably called upon to serve on committees. Shaw actually enjoyed committee work, and learned a great deal about human nature in the process. He also learned how to get his own way. Often he sat through stormy sessions, patiently waiting for the proper moment to submit the plan he had devised long in advance. Shaw said, only half facetiously, that the only people who saw much of him were those who served on committees with him.[4]

It is unlikely that anyone else in London had so much as passing acquaintance with so many different shades of heretics. Shaw took it for granted that the various circles which he inhabited did not themselves intersect. "As my friends lived in different worlds and I rarely introduced one to the other they did not necessarily know one another."[5]

Once at the Hall of Science when he was still a novice, Shaw, sitting far back in the Hall, rose to make a comment after a lecture by Charles Bradlaugh. He had scarcely uttered two sentences, when the great secularist rose and said, "The gentleman is a speaker. Come to the platform." Shaw reports that he did so and that Bradlaugh devoted considerable time to a reply. But he never formally debated Bradlaugh. He was once scheduled to do so on behalf of William Morris's Socialist League on the subject, "Will Socialism benefit the English people?" Bradlaugh insisted that socialism be defined in Hyndman's terms, and as H. M. Hyndman was strongly anti-Fabian, Shaw refused. The debate was called off – Shaw admits to his relief at the time, though later he regretted the lost opportunity. History regrets it too. "It pleases me to imagine," Shaw mused, "that he refused a set debate with me much as Edmund Kean refused to act with Macready." But this was wishful thinking. Bradlaugh, in those days, was taking on all comers. Shaw did debate with Bradlaugh's successor, G. W. Foote, after Bradlaugh's death. "We went at it hammer-and-tongs for two nights. Oratorically honors were even; but I was more at home in economics than Foote, and should, I believe, have won the verdict had a vote been taken."[6]

Shaw's most personal link with organized secularism was, of course, through Annie Besant whom he literally wooed from the influence of Charles Bradlaugh and Edward Aveling into the Fabian Society in 1885. Though she had formerly supported Bradlaugh's anti-socialist position in his debates with H. M. Hyndman, Mrs. Besant now claimed that socialism and secularism were thoroughly compatible. Shaw's victory (if so he considered it) was short-lived. He was as puzzled as Bradlaugh was pained at her sudden conversion to theosophy by Mme. Helena Blavatsky in 1889. Shaw himself claims to have given her Blavatsky's *The Secret Doctrine* to review for W. T. Stead's paper after he had found it virtually unreadable. When he heard of her conversion, he rushed around to the Secular Society's shop to ask if she was quite mad. "It was no use," Shaw wrote 40 years later. "She actually joked about it, a thing I never heard her do before. She said she supposed that since she had, as a Theosophist, become a vegetarian, her mind may have been affected."[7] Out of loyalty she remained an editor of *The National Reformer* until Bradlaugh's death.

After Annie and most of her cohorts had died, Shaw ventured an explanation:

> Like all great public speakers, she was a born actress. She was successively a Puseyite Evangelical, an Atheist Bible Smasher, a Darwinian Secularist, a Fabian Socialist, a Strike Leader, and finally a Theosophist, exactly as Mrs. Siddons was Lady Macbeth, Lady Randolph, Beatrice, Rosalind, and Volumnia. She "saw herself" as a priestess above all: that was how Theosophy held her to the end. There was a different leading man every time: Bradlaugh, Robertson, Aveling, Shaw, and Herbert Burrows. That did not matter. Whoever does not understand this, as I, a playwright, do, will never understand the career of Annie Besant.[8]

Shaw had other acquaintances among the freethought fraternity. In 1882 Edward Bibbins Aveling began to frequent the Reading Room of the British Museum, which was practically a club for impoverished intellectuals. Bernard Shaw, still in relative obscurity was in regular attendance, and he had already made the acquaintance there of Eleanor Marx, youngest of Karl's daughters, whom he found attractive and stimulating. Eleanor (called "Tussy") and Shaw were also both members of the Browning Society. This relationship was companionate and perhaps flirtatious, nothing more. I do not know if Shaw actually introduced Aveling to Eleanor. In any case, Aveling recalled having previously met her when she was a young girl in the company of her father.

Aveling, a man of many parts, is known chiefly to the world as the model for the artistic scoundrel, Louis Dubedat, in Shaw's *The Doctor's Dilemma*. It is possible that a good deal of the surrounding material may have found its way into the play as well. But Shaw used these materials, as he always did, for his own ends, and the picture of Louis Dubedat as charming and personable and as an artist of undeniable genius must not be confused with the real Edward Aveling. Aveling's field was science and he was for a time Bradlaugh's science editor for *The National Reformer*, but he had a great store of literary and artistic knowledge as well. He turned down a permanent chair at King's College, London University, because it required church membership. He served on the London School Board. He once managed a traveling theatrical troupe. Shaw found him "quite a pleasant fellow, who would have gone to the stake for Socialism or atheism, but with absolutely no conscience in his private life. And though no woman seemed able to resist him he was short, with the face and eyes of a lizard, and no physical charm except a voice like a euphonium."[9]

For a time Annie Besant was on the most intimate terms with Aveling. Interestingly, as Aveling became more and more interested in Tussy Marx, Annie Besant found Shaw more and more attractive, until, at length, she joined the Fabian Society.

Shaw did introduce Aveling to the humanitarian, Henry Salt, and his wife. Salt was surprised to find a scientific socialist so emotional and sentimental. Aveling liked to read aloud, and when he read the last act of Shelley's *Prometheus Unbound*, "he trembled and shook in his passionate excitement and then burst into sobs and tears." Although Shelley was his great love, he was nearly turned down, for personal reasons, for membership in the Shelley Society. Shaw assured the circle that "if it came to giving one's life for a cause, one could rely on Aveling even if he carried all our purses with him to the scaffold."[10]

The Marx-Aveling affair had far more tragic consequences than any that Shaw portrayed in *The Doctor's Dilemma*. Eleanor's life with Aveling was miserable, and ended, sixteen years after their meeting, in her suicide. Actually, Aveling, like Louis Dubedat, was stricken in health and handed over to the care of a prominent physician, Edward Heath – who successfully saved the scoundrel's life, much to the dismay of Tussy's many friends. Lewis Feuer assumes also (though Shaw never said so) that Jennifer Dubedat is a picture of Eleanor Marx.[11] In any case, Shaw knew both of them quite well, and Feuer is right, I think, in observing that no other of Shaw's women lives with such complete passion. And this is not out of keeping with the impression of Tussy we get from Havelock Ellis, who had ample opportunity to observe her, since she was the close friend of both Olive Schreiner, who did not quite become his wife, and Edith M. O. Lees, who eventually did.

In 1882, the same year in which Shaw first met Aveling, a traveling Scottish philosopher, Thomas Davidson, was gathering interested Londoners in his rooms to talk about religion, ethics, and social reform – the beginning of the London branch of the Fellowship of the New Life. This lively discussion group eventually split over the insoluble question as to whether personal regeneration must come before social reform. The social reformers broke away from the regenerators and became in 1884 the Fabian Society.

Shaw, in his *Fabian Essays*, recounts the split, but does not mention by name either the Fellowship or Davidson. Indeed, he gives the impression here and elsewhere that he knew nothing of the Fabian Society until he attended an early meeting of it. Yet he must have attended at least one Fellowship meeting previously. He reported years later to Henry Salt that when the "learned Scottish professor" discoursed on "the cultivation of a perfect character," the audience fell into such bewildered silence that the Chairman turned finally to Shaw to break it. Dutifully Shaw said that his mind was a perfect blank and that he had been "bored as he had never been bored before." Shaw remained remorseful about this outburst, and in after years when Davidson sent him a copy of his new book, he meant to atone for his former insult by writing a "pleasant" review. "But when I looked into the book I felt all my old feelings return."[12]

In spite of the human flaw that engendered such antipathies, Davidson set loose sufficient energies in his Chelsea rooms, to keep a self-improvement society in existence for a decade and a half, many of whose members remained on the rolls of the Fabian Society as well.

In the eighties and nineties there were heretics within the Church as well as outside it, and it should come as no real surprise to any student of Shaw to find that he was often more sympathetic to the liberal clergy than he was to the atheistic movement. Chief among such clergy within the Establishment was the founder and leader of the Christian Socialist Guild of Saint Matthew, Stewart D. Headlam. Headlam, in endless trouble with his Bishops because of his socialism, his defense of the stage, and his modernist reading of the scriptures, was for many years denied a pulpit, but remained an influential force within the Church through the Guild and through his outspoken editorship of *The Church Reformer*. He was a fellow Fabian, but he did not always follow Shaw's lead. They never became intimate friends. There has always been speculation about how much of Headlam went into the character of the Christian Socialist clergyman, James Mavor Morell, in Shaw's *Candida* in 1895, though Shaw took some pains to point out that Morell was closer to Stopford Brooke with touches of Canon Shuttleworth and Fleming Williams. In the early days Shaw used the Guild of Saint Matthew, as he used every other possible opportunity, to practise his public speaking. Many years later, when Headlam was again in relatively good grace with the Bishop of London, Shaw's address to the Guild in Essex Hall on "Some Necessary Repairs to Religion" once more disturbed the delicate equilibrium. No doubt it was inadequately reported, but the statement that "there is no established religion on the earth today in which an intelligent and educated man can believe," was hotly contested by, among others, G. K. Chesterton. The Bishop of London asked for – and got – Headlam's formal repudiation of any of Shaw's statements that were in contradiction to the Christian faith; but at a later meeting of the Guild, Headlam made a formal reply to critics of Shaw's speech.[13] It was obvious that Headlam was not shocked by Shaw. "He believes in the Holy Ghost, and if he says a word against the Son of Man, it is mainly against false conceptions, and it shall be forgiven him."[14]

One of Shaw's recollections was of Headlam's fierce temper and of his resolve to control it, causing him sometimes to go white in public. At Fabian meetings he never spoke directly about religion, but Shaw tried to understand the religious and artistic side of him. Headlam was "mystically Catholic," Shaw felt, "rather than industrially Collectivist."[15]

Few others tried to probe the sensitive artistic side of this outspoken and apparently extroverted religious reformer, and it is possible that Headlam did not rightly understand it himself. When, in the midst of his troubles with the Establishment, friends suggested that he might be happier in some nonconformist sect, he was genuinely shocked. The ritual and sacraments of High Church were more meaningful to him than its creeds. The artistic sensibilities, of which only his intimates could have been aware, were poignantly sharpened by the disaster of his marriage. It was so catastrophic that his biographer, writing only two years after Headlam's death, would not discuss it or even mention the lady's name – Beatrice Pennington. The 1878 marriage lasted "a few years" and ended in painful frustration when it became apparent that Beatrice had a penchant for homosexuality. Afterwards, in good Victorian convention, the marriage was simply not mentioned. Years after all the principals were dead, Shaw mentioned the truth casually in the preface to another man's book.[16]

The centre of London nonconformity was City Temple on Holborn Viaduct, which for many years had rung with the vaguely liberal oratory of Joseph Parker. But the thundering Parker had never created such a stir as the slight, poetic, spiritual figure who succeeded him in 1902. Rev. Reginald J. Campbell probably preached to the largest congregations ever assembled regularly in Central London – if we leave out of account such temporary phenomena as the revivalist meetings of Moody and Sankey. Campbell was also a socialist, but not a vigorous

Fabian, and it was not his social gospel that drew thousands of Londoners to hear him and caused tumults within the citadel of Congregationalism.

Campbell was London's first really popular modernist in interpreting the scriptures. His pulpit style retained the conventions of his time – "Yea, verily ... Nay ... Think you this, brethren ... ." And he was fond of quoting from poems and hymns, all of which he did quite effectively. But beneath this disarming surface he gave his congregation a mystical, rational combination close to the views of Ernest Renan or Moncure Conway. What was acceptable from his pulpit, however, proved far more shocking in print. And particularly after the publication of his *The New Theology* in 1907 he became the centre of a theological storm, which did not completely subside until, in ill health and deeply distressed by the outbreak of World War I, Campbell withdrew his book from publication, took orders in the Anglican Church, and permanently left the London scene in 1915.

At City Temple Campbell dealt with the "spiritual Christ" not the "historical Jesus" whom the Continental critics were trying vainly to rediscover. He spoke of Christ as a "divine impulse" that summed up everything that was good. "Instead of thinking about rules of service, we think about Him, and thus we are compelled towards the goodness which ever recedes as we approach it, which is a spirit rather than a code."[17] In his first Christmas sermon he made it clear that incarnation meant not only that God became man, but that man is becoming God, that humanity progresses towards the godhead. This is, in fact, the creative evolution of Henri Bergson which Bernard Shaw had adapted to his religion of the Life Force. This was the heresy which Stewart Headlam was required to repudiate when Shaw spoke for the GSM at Essex Hall in 1906. The week before (on 22 November) Shaw had said much the same thing at City Temple's Literary Society in "The Religion of the British Empire."[18] Campbell had no bishop to instruct him in the matter, but on the Sunday following, his full sermon ("The Modes of

God") was a commentary on Shaw's remarks. Shaw, without calling himself a Christian, had, said the minister, grasped the central principle of the gospel with a firm hand.

Campbell and Shaw remained on friendly terms, at least up until World War I. Shaw spoke at the City Temple Literary Society at least four times, and *The Christian Commonwealth* (its unofficial organ) gave space, in addition, to speeches he made elsewhere. Some public altercation arose when the *Commonwealth* on 14 October 1908 featured a banner headline on the first page: "How I Came To Believe in Christ by G. Bernard Shaw." Perusal of his actual words, however, quickly reveals that GBS had not been converted to Christianity! He had said that Mr. Campbell had finally placed before him a figure of Christ in which an educated man living in the twentieth century could believe, and a person whose ideas were worth examining. Nevertheless, one secular journalist described Shaw as "crawling to the feet of Jesus." The public dialogue between Shaw and Campbell on the nature of Jesus continued for some time.

Only one other figure besides Shaw wove himself consistently into the pattern of London heresies without becoming committed to any of them. That person was William T. Stead, editor of the *Pall Mall Gazette* and the *Review of Reviews*. He and Shaw were, each in his own way, such incurable reformers and such compulsive meddlers that few London groups calling themselves "progressive" did not know them.

Stead and Shaw were not a team. They rarely saw each other over the three decades when they were both in London, but they did communicate occasionally.[19] Stead indirectly gave Shaw needed assistance in the beginning of his journalistic career, leading to a continuing association of Shaw with the *Pall Mall Gazette*. Shaw supported Stead's anti-slum and anti-war drives, but their aims were never identical. They were not compatible personally. "He was a gifted journalist," Shaw wrote of Stead, "but a complete Philistine, to whom literature was not a fine art but simply news. He was as ignorant as it is possible for a newspaper man in possession of his five senses to be on art, science, philosophy; in short of literature."[20] Neither had Stead any understanding of the "new morality" – especially sex morality – and his warm friendship with such "new women" as Annie Besant and Olive Schreiner remains something of a mystery. His crusades against sin and against war were the most flamboyant London had ever seen. Still, standing on the deck of the *Titanic,* at the sensational end to a sensational career, there was some doubt as to whether he had changed London more than London had changed him.

The time came when Shaw's life became too full for constant public speaking. He had not time to prepare new presentations and was afraid of becoming "a windbag with only one speech." About 1895 he began to limit his public appearances to special occasions.

Shaw was unique among the London heretics in that he had developed his own substitute religion, really his own theology. Although his reputation steadily grew as the great idol smasher, he made it a point always to have replacements for the broken crockery. Too often, with the help of the GBS-jokester, the smashing ceremony was such fun, and provided such welcome release, that no one really investigated the worth of the new article. As recently as 1960, to mark the tenth anniversary of Shaw's death, the *New York Times Magazine* presented a page of Shavian paradoxes completely out of context, simply as jokes, with no overtones of the prophetic voice. Eric Bentley, in 1947, was among the first to point out in so many words that the comic puppet which Shaw so skillfully constructed to win him an audience, turned on the old sage and almost overcame him.[21] In vain Peter Keegan (in *John Bull's Other Island*) cried out, "Every dream is a prophecy: every jest is an earnest in the womb of Time."

There was for Shaw none of the early suffering that so many of his contemporaries experienced in breaking from the old faith.

He was born and baptized in the Established Church of Ireland (like Father George Tyrrell), but his mother, he tells us, had been brought up so strictly that, in reaction, church-going was dropped in his family before he was ten years old. He considered himself a sceptic from early childhood. He did feel, for a time, disposed to say prayers. "I cannot recall the final form I adopted; but I remember that it was in three movements, like a sonata, and in the best Church of Ireland style. It ended with the Lord's Prayer; and I repeated it every night in bed."[22]

He was never confirmed. He does not think his parents were either. Irish Protestantism was for him not a religion at all, but a social convention. His few exposures to it were not for the sake of his own salvation, but for his father's respectability. When they went to live at Torca Cottage on Dalkey Hill in 1866, all religious practice was discontinued.

> Imagine being taught that there is one God, a Protestant and perfect gentleman, keeping Heaven select for the gentry against an idolatrous imposter called the Pope! Imagine the pretensions of the English peerage on the incomes of the English middle class! I remember Stopford Brooke one day telling me that he discerned in my books an intense and contemptuous hatred for society. No wonder![23]

His revolt against the church was of a piece with his revolt against society. When he was too young to be allowed out by himself, a nurse was dispatched to take him for a walk in some nicer neighbourhood. Instead, the servant would meet a male acquaintance and the three of them would go into a public house where he was treated with lemonade or gingerbeer. But young Shaw knew that his own father's life had been made miserable by drink, and looked upon the public house as a wicked place. "Thus were laid the foundations of my lifelong hatred of poverty, and the devotion of all my public life to the task of exterminating the poor and rendering their resurrection for ever impossible."[24] Shaw's humour never concealed the bitterness he felt about his early years. He would have been more decently brought up, he maintains, if his parents had been too poor to afford servants.[25]

It is not surprising, then, to find the adult Shaw in London proclaiming himself an atheist. But, as he later pointed out, there are several kinds of atheism. "There is the youthful Atheism with which every able modern mind begins: an Atheism that clears the soul of superstitions and terrors and servilities and base compliances and hypocrisies, and lets in the light of heaven. And then there is the Atheism of despair and pessimism."[26] It was the former kind Shaw subscribed to when he shocked some of the ladies of the Shelley Society by proclaiming that he was, like Shelley, a socialist, an atheist, and a vegetarian. Besides, this was in the days when the opposition to Bradlaugh and Foote had achieved such proportions that Shaw would rather have been counted among their supporters than among their attackers. "I preferred to call myself an Atheist because belief in God meant belief in the old tribal idol called Jehovah; and I would not, by calling myself an Agnostic, pretend that I did not know whether it existed or not."[27]

But socialism alone was not enough. It was precisely H. M. Hyndman's limitation that he never went beyond Marx and internationalism. "He never went on from the industrial revolution to the next things – to the revolution in morals, and to the formulation and establishment of a credible and effective indigenous Western religion."[28] Shaw found Bradlaugh's survivors in the National Secular Society to be, in this regard, "Freethought Fundamentalists," unable to accept even the poetic imagery of mysticism. Their position remained essentially one of denial, Shaw felt; and although this position had been forced upon Bradlaugh by the nature of his pioneering campaigns against the Establishment, the time had come for affirmation.

Since there was no affirmative religion in the Western World in which a reasonably intelligent man could believe, Shaw proceeded to devise one for himself. He enjoyed using old words in fresh ways, and one can find him calling himself a Catholic at one point and a Protestant at another. He used the word "Catholic" to mean "universal" (it meant the same as "communist," he said). When he called himself Protestant, he thought of himself as a Separatist from the Establishment. "Now of Separation there is no end until every human being is a Separate Church, for which there is much to be said."[29] His aim, therefore, was a belief that could be at the same time individual and universal. Scattered statements of this sort have led the unwary to suppose that Shaw's religious beliefs kept fluctuating in order to produce the best paradox at any given moment. Instead, his religion, as it matured, formed a steadying and consistent strain in one of the most complex minds of the twentieth century. That complexity involved such unexplored wells of despair and such extremes of what is presently called "existential pain," that even now the Shavian playgoer, still watched over and protected by the GBS-jokester, has never had more than a glimpse within. But that is a matter for another time.

It goes without saying that any religion devised by Shaw would have to complement his socialism. It would have to be, therefore, concerned with justice and the social order and the improvement of life on this planet. Yet a purely pragmatist approach did not appeal to him. Pragmatism tended to maintain that whatever works is good, and he perceived that many systems that produced some good results were inherently evil. Napoleon, for instance, brought many beneficent changes to Europe, yet it would have been better for the world if he had never been born. Shaw preferred a mystical revelation to a rationalist one. He says he abandoned rationalism after his second novel – which would have been in 1880.

Neither could he accept the whole cult of science, nor the scientist as the new priest. He was forced to accept the fact of evolution, but he rebelled, with Samuel Butler, against the idea of "the survival of the fittest," if by that was meant a cosmos governed by mere accident. He preferred the earlier evolutionary theory of Chevalier de Lamarck, which permitted the presence of mind or will in the evolutionary process. Whereas Darwinians might assume that the giraffe had a long neck because, in an area where the only available food was ever higher in the trees, only those lucky enough to have a "neck-advantage" could survive and breed, Shaw and Butler would have argued that only those animals with sufficient will to stretch their necks a little farther would survive. The results in both instances would be the same, but the conception of the nature of life, wholly different.

What then, was the source of this will that ran through all living things? Shaw preferred the term and the conception of Henri Bergson – the *Élan Vital*, the Life Force. He sometimes called it the evolutionary appetite. He did not like to call it God, though occasionally, for City Temple audiences, he did so with careful stipulations. It was more proper, perhaps, to call it the Holy Spirit ("the only surviving member of the Trinity"). Near the end of his life he consented to refer to it as Divine Providence.

The familiar terminology may be initially disarming, but his readers and listeners soon discovered (and in some cases were all the more shocked) that the Life Force, by whatever name, had few of the attributes usually associated with godhead. It had no "personality." It was not omnipotent. It was not necessarily beneficent. But it was persistent. It had a direction. It was moving toward godhead and would continue so to move indefinitely. At first this may seem to have been a kind of unjustifiable optimism on Shaw's part, but, if so, it was optimism only on a cosmic plane. For there was no guarantee that the human race as we know it, or even that this planet as we know it, would succeed in being a proper instrument of the Life Force. Indeed as Shaw grew older, there seemed to be more and more evidence that we would be "scrapped." When Lawrence Langner of the Theatre Guild brought Shaw greetings from Eugene O'Neill (whom he had never met), Shaw politely inquired about O'Neill's health and state of mind. Langner reported that O'Neill was pessimistic about the state of the world and was of the opinion that our present civilization was on its way downhill and headed for ultimate disaster. " 'Tell him not to worry about that,' said Shaw cheerily. 'If mankind turns out, as I suspect, to be a failure, it will destroy itself and be replaced by some other creature.' "[30]

Shaw's oft-vaunted optimism turns out to be, on closer examination, a combination of good health, cheerfulness, and a remarkable kind of detachment. Furthermore, he was constitutionally opposed to cynicism. He could see no point in continually addressing a dying civilization. Unlike a later Irish expatriate, Samuel Beckett, he made the assumption that there were those in his audiences and among his readers who could be stirred to action by his message and might rescue our tottering civilization from the abyss. "We live," he said in one of those remarkably Shavian images, "as in a villa on Vesuvius."[31]

Hence, the tone of the schoolmaster and the preacher: we must set our house in order, eliminate poverty, and learn government, so we may have at least an off-chance for survival. But this is rudimentary. Our real aim must be to become more sentient beings, longer lived, and more abundantly alive, so that we can carry out the will of the Life Force. The Life Force has no hands or mind of its own. When he spoke of these matters in public, the familiar GBS-jokester vanished, and audiences described as "consternated" or even "terrified" heard him say,

> If you don't do his work it won't be done; if you turn away from it, if you sit down and say, "Thy will be done," you might as well be the most irreligious person on the face of the earth. But if you will stand by your God, if you will say, "My business is to do your will, my hands are your hands, my tongue is your tongue, my brain is your brain, I am here to do thy work, and I will do it," you will get rid of otherworldliness, you will get rid of all that religion which is made an excuse and a cloak for doing nothing, and you will learn not only to worship your God, but also to have a fellow feeling with him.[32]

After that, it is not too difficult to accept his repeated claim to affinity with the Society of Friends. "If I had to be fitted into any religious denomination, the Society of Friends ... would have the best chance," he once explained to newspaper questioning.[33] But he went on to say at once that in the face of his very explicit writings on the subject there is no excuse for regarding him as a member of any church or sect, "unless the believers in Creative Evolution can be described as a sect." I know of no instance where Shaw ever attended a Quaker Meeting for Worship or in any way identified himself with the Society of Friends as an organization. He was attracted to their method of silent worship, their dependence on "the inner light" (a phrase he occasionally borrowed), and their courageous pacifism at the time of World War I. In later years he became particularly interested in the life of the Quaker founder, George Fox, and included him in the cast of characters of *In Good King Charles's Golden Days*.

The essay, "What Is My Religious Faith?" in *Sixteen Self Sketches* is capsule size. His most complete exposition is the 86-page Preface to *Back to Methuselah*. But the theme is unmistakable in all his works, especially from *Man and Superman* (1903) onwards. His most perceptive critics – G. K. Chesterton, J. S. Collis, C. E. M. Joad, Eric Bentley – have dealt seriously with his religion. And it is encouraging to note that a younger commentator, Anthony S. Abbott, has published a study of *Shaw and Christianity*.[34]

Bernard Shaw, like his old friend, Annie Besant, was destined to live many "lives" – author, journalist, orator, politician, committee man, man of the world, and so forth – as he himself has enumerated them. They were held together, more securely than Annie's, by his twin beliefs in socialism and the Life Force. First one, then the other, grew from the spiritual turmoil of the London into which he consciously threw himself during his first decade there. Both served to sustain him through the longest and most productive of the many careers that emerged from that same crucible.

NOTES

1 Archibald Henderson, *George Bernard Shaw: Man of the Century* (New York, 1956), pp. 135–9.

2 C. M. Davies, *Heterodox London*, 2 vols. (London, 1874) I: 178.
3 See G. B. Shaw, "How I Became a Public Speaker," *Sixteen Self Sketches* (London, 1949), p. 56.
4 *Sixteen Self Sketches*, p. 130.
5 Stephen Winsten, *Salt and His Circle* (London, 1951), preface, p. 13.
6 *Sixteen Self Sketches*, pp. 61–2.
7 Bernard Shaw to The Editor of *The Freethinker*, n.d., the Berg Collection.
8 *Ibid.*
9 Bernard Shaw to L. Preger, 22 February 1946, the Berg Collection.
10 Winsten, pp. 83–4.
11 Lewis Feuer, "The Marxian Tragedians," *Encounter*, XIX, 5 (1962): 23–32.
12 Winsten, Appendix I, p. 207.
13 *The Times*, London, 30 November, 7 December, 22 December 1906.
14 Frederick G. Bettany, *Stewart Headlam* (London, 1926), p. 89.
15 *Ibid.*, p. 139.
16 Winsten, p. 9.
17 R. J. Campbell, *City Temple Sermons* (London, 1903), pp. 194–5.
18 See W. S. Smith, ed., *The Religious Speeches of Bernard Shaw* (University Park, Pa., 1963).
19 See Patrick G. Hogan, Jr., and Joseph O. Baylen, "G. Bernard Shaw and W. T. Stead; An Unexplored Relationship," *Studies in English Literature* 1500–1900, I (Autumn, 1961): 123–47.
20 GBS to the Editor, *The Freethinker*, *loc. cit.*
21 Eric Bentley, *Bernard Shaw* (New York, 1957). See especially part IV "The Fool in Christ."
22 Bernard Shaw, Preface to *Immaturity*, Standard Edition (London, 1931), pp. xviii–xix.
23 *Sixteen Self Sketches*, p. 46.
24 Preface to *London Music in 1888–89*, Standard Edition (London, 1937), p. 13.
25 The most detailed treatment of Shaw's early years, some of it speculative, is in B. C. Rosset, *Shaw of Dublin* (University Park, Pa., 1964).
26 G. B. Shaw, *What I Really Wrote About the War* (New York, 1932), p. 84.
27 *Sixteen Self Sketches*, p. 74.
28 G. B. Shaw, *Pen Portraits and Reviews*, in a review of Hyndman's Memoirs, Standard Edition (London, 1932), p. 128.
29 G. B. Shaw "How William Archer Impressed Bernard Shaw," *Pen Portraits and Reviews*, p. 4.
30 L. Langner, *G.B.S. and the Lunatic* (New York, 1963), p. 5.
31 G. B. Shaw, *The Intelligent Woman's Guide to Socialism and Capitalism*, Standard Edition (London, 1932), p. 302.
32 W. S. Smith, ed., *Religious Speeches ...*, pp. 6–7.
33 Blanche Patch, *Thirty Years With Bernard Shaw* (New York, 1951), p. 227. See my article, "Bernard Shaw and the Quakers," *Bulletin of Friends Historical Association*, XLV, 2: 105.
34 The Seabury Press, New York, 1965.

JAMES D. MERRITT

Shaw and the Pre-Raphaelites

To discuss Shaw and the pre-Raphaelites is to discuss Shaw as a late nineteenth-century art critic, as a socialist, and finally as the author of *Candida*. I do not wish to suggest that the pre-Raphaelites and pre-Raphaelitism were profound or life-long influences upon Shaw, but I would like to emphasize certain connections that appear to have been largely ignored or, it seems to me, too little appreciated. My purpose is to add one more pebble to the mountain of Shaw scholarship.

The significance of the pre-Raphaelites lies in the fact that it was a unique movement in Victorian England in that it embraced poetry, painting, household decoration, architecture and design of all kinds as related elements. Because it went beyond painting and the written word, it to some extent touched on political thought as well. In a century full of major revolutions it is a comparatively small one, but pre-Raphaelites such as Rossetti and the young Swinburne helped to establish new tastes in art which were the foundation upon which much of contemporary taste is based. Their contempt for Victorian middle-class taste was a forerunner of the all-out revolt against middle-class taste which has been the hallmark of so much of art since 1848. They were the artists and poets who opened the door for aestheticism of the nineties in the English-speaking world. Aestheticism in turn, of course, opened the door for all of the movements that have aimed at shocking the bourgeois since that time. It is not too much to see them as the first modern group of artists in

England. The young pre-Raphaelites were the first English-speaking bohemian artists.

At the risk of repeating some fairly familiar literary and art history I am going to attempt to summarize the history and significance of the Pre-Raphaelite Movement. Its genesis was a combination of two powerful forces in early nineteenth-century intellectual history: the spread of Romanticism in the world of art, and the evangelical spirit, which did so much to reform, or perhaps one should say revise, the Protestant Church. From the Romantics the pre-Raphaelites derived their love of a mysterious past, a Gothic past as opposed to a classical past, and a yearning to somehow avoid the ugliness of industrialized, pragmatic, Philistine Victorian England. From certain of the Romantics they inherited as well a tendency towards a kind of amorphous idealism in which such abstractions as concepts of purity played a role. From the evangelical spirit of the late eighteenth and early nineteenth centuries they inherited a zeal for reform; they wanted to reform art chiefly, but some of them, such as William Morris, wanted to reform the political and economic systems of England as well. Ironically, their aims at reform were often based upon a return to the past. Archibald Henderson has summarized Shaw's opinion of the achievements of two of them very neatly: "He [Shaw] maintained that William Morris made himself the greatest living master of the English language, both in prose and verse, by picking up the tradition of the literary art where Chaucer left it; that Burne-Jones made himself the greatest among English decorative painters by picking up the tradition of his art where Lippi left it, and utterly ignoring their Raphaels, Correggios and stuff."[1] Shaw was not, of course, saying that art had not had any significance since Raphael or that literature had ceased to exist since Chaucer; he was merely restating the pre-Raphaelite belief that English art and literature had spent several centuries in wasted efforts at continuing the traditions of the Renaissance while ignoring the achievements of the pre-Renaissance artists. What seemed to the Victorians to be primitive, seemed to the pre-Raphaelites, and to Shaw, to have a purity and realism that Renaissance art did not have.

To be more specific: the predecessors of the pre-Raphaelites were a group of German painters who settled in Rome at the end of the first decade of the nineteenth century. They established a brotherhood which was semi-monastic in character in which ritualistic prayer played a role nearly as large as that played by painting. There is an interesting look at a Nazarene painter in George Eliot's *Middlemarch*, for it is the studio of one of these painters that is visited by Dorothea during her honeymoon in Rome with Mr. Casaubon. George Eliot treats the young artist with a rather tongue-in-cheek tone, but there were other Englishmen who did not. The most important of these was Ford Madox Brown who saw the work of the Nazarenes on a visit to Rome in 1845. Brown was a very important man in the Pre-Raphaelite Movement. A historian of the movement refers to him as its "virtual founder"[2] and another asserts that "the Pre-Raphaelites probably learnt more [from him] than from anyone else."[3] I emphasize this connection between Brown and the pre-Raphaelites because Shaw was a great admirer of Brown's painting and went so far as to compare his work most favourably with that of Ibsen. Brown, said Shaw in 1897, "had vitality enough to find intense enjoyment in the world as it really is, unbeautified, unidealized, unvitiated in any way for artistic consumption."[4] Shaw admired the realism in Brown's work, in other words. The introduction of the word realism leads us to the next step in the founding of the Pre-Raphaelite Movement.

Three young painters, Dante Gabriel Rossetti, John Everett Millais, and William Holman Hunt were the trinity upon which it was all founded. They were fairly disgusted by the taste of the late forties. The Academy was dominated by academicians. There seems to have been general agreement among them that Raphael and other painters of the High Renaissance were to be seen as the ultimate standards of perfection; they may be said to have been pro-Raphael. Rossetti, Millais, and Holman Hunt felt that the precision of Raphael's settings and the almost geometrical arrangement of the subjects was unrealistic and unnatural; they decided that their painting would be the very opposite. It would be realistic and natural. Rossetti had already been a student of Ford Madox Brown's and had seen examples of the spare, almost photographic style that Brown had developed. When he came across a book of engravings showing some frescoes in Pisa done by painters who pre-dated Raphael, he and his friends found a focus for their ideas. They would use these early Italian masters as examples; their paintings would be in a pre-Raphaelite style. Its chief characteristics would be great attention to detail, a tendency towards simplicity in execution, and a real attempt to be realistic. They formed a secret brotherhood along with four other friends and the famous PRB was born. Right from the start it was a movement that sought to flaunt the authority of the academicians. At first all of the artists eschewed anything that might be construed as commercial. They seriously believed that art could make life better and more beautiful.

Despite their belief in "strict actuality" there is something dreamy and unrealistic about a lot of the early pre-Raphaelite paintings. Looking at those early paintings one can see that pre-Raphaelitism was a paradoxical movement right from the start. It sought to be realistic, to be pure, to bring beauty into a Philistine world, to be a force for betterment. But their subject matter, for one thing, was a problem. They liked to do illustrations from Shakespeare's plays, or Keats' poems, or from the Bible. They often used their friends and relatives as models, thus establishing a tie between past and present, reality and fancy, but it is a tenuous connection. Shaw was to compare the pre-Raphaelites with the Christian socialists in his *Preface to Pleasant Plays*.

To return to specifics: the pre-Raphaelites started a small journal, which was symbolically named *The Germ*. Unfortunately it lasted for only four issues, a strange little magazine full of poetry, papers about art, and essays on aesthetics. If there is a unifying element in the material in *The Germ* it is an attempt to abide by "the principle of strict actuality" to use William Michael Rossetti's phrase. Some of the poems are of the sort that aroused the ire of the good Scot, Robert Buchanan, who attacked certain poems as "fleshly" because they seemed to extol the pleasures of the body over the more abstract delights of the spirit. Shaw obviously found them "fleshly" too. Miss Janet Dunbar, in her biography of Charlotte Shaw, quotes from a letter written by Mrs. Shaw to Siegfried Trebitsch in which "G.B.S. wishes to know if the poetry of Dante Gabriel Rossetti and Swinburne is known in Germany, as Wilde's *Salome* should not appear extraordinary – quite the contrary – to anyone familiar with the poets of the Pre-Raphaelite Movement."[5] The poems of Rossetti do not seem particularly shocking today and Swinburne's early poems are not shockers anymore, though Wilde's play still seems fairly shocking – at least it did recently to some of my own students. Rossetti and Swinburne (and other of the pre-Raphaelite poets) were shocking in their day because they appeared to celebrate love that was not blessed by the Church and that did not have as its end the establishment of a household. It is, of course, a truism to say that Victorian society was based upon the home and the family. The pre-Raphaelites were not very interested in home and the family; they were sensualists and their love of sensuality is evident in the intense love of colour in their paintings as well as in the subject matter of their poetry.

Side by side with the "fleshly" poems, however, one can find the mystical and deeply religious poetry of such pre-Raphaelite figures as Christina Rossetti and James Collinson. These poems are full of a yearning for salvation and evidence of devout faith. In reading these poems one can see the paradox of pre-Raphaelitism and that it was going in several directions at once. Along with the poems written by poets sowing their wild oats are the poems that show the evangelical spirit of the Nazarenes.

Although *The Germ* failed after only a few months, its influence was fairly widespread and it was not very long before the pre-Raphaelites were widely known – and ridiculed. The first pre-Raphaelite paintings that the public saw received very rough treatment from the critics, both professional and amateur. Dickens, for example, was so disgusted by a picture of Millais's that he called it "mean, odious, repulsive and revolting." The picture, incidentally, showed the child Jesus in the carpenter's shop. For Joseph, Millais had used an actual carpenter as a model and he showed the child Jesus as a very real looking little boy with rather splay feet that were not very clean. It is an unprettified, realistic picture. Ford Madox Brown's pictures, also, were extremely realistic. Shaw admired him enormously as a realist and said of him that he was "the most dramatic of all painters." Like Ibsen, his themes were "not youth, beauty, morality, gentility and prosperity as conceived by Mr. Smith of Brixton and Bayswater, but real life taken as it is, with no more regard for poor Smith's dreams and hypocrisies than the weather has for his shiny silk hat when he forgets his umbrella." Shaw goes on to flail Mr. Smith and prevailing middle class taste in art:

> This love of life and knowledge of its worth is a rare thing – whole Alps and Andes above the common demand for prettiness, fashionableness, refinement, elegance of style, delicacy of sentiment, charm of character, sympathetic philosophy (the philosophy of the happy ending), decorative moral systems contrasting roseate and rapturous vice with lilied and langorous virtue, and making "Love" face both ways as the universal softener and redeemer, the whole being worshipped as beauty or virtue, and set in place of life to narrow and condition it instead of enlarging and fulfilling it. To such self-indulgence most artists are mere pandars for the sense of beauty needed to make an artist is so strong that the sense of life in him must needs be quite prodigious to overpower it. It must always be a mystery to the ordinary beauty-fancying, life-shrinking amateur how the realist in art can bring his unbeautified, remorseless celebrations of common life in among so many pretty, pleasant, sweet, noble,

touching fictions and yet take his place among the highest, although the railing, the derision, the protest, the positive disgust are almost universal at first.[6]

Shaw went on to compare Brown and Rembrandt and decided that Brown is always a realist whereas Rembrandt is a realist only in his drawing: "he [Rembrandt] would draw life with perfect integrity, but would paint it with a golden glow."

In this same review, which, incidentally, is a review of two plays and not of an exhibition, Shaw also speaks of G. F. Watts, another pre-Raphaelite painter, but one of the pre-Raphaelites who emphasized the idealistic rather than the realistic. Watts paints "a visionary world in which life fades into mist and the imaginings of nobility and beauty with which we invest life becomes embodied and visible."[7]

Shaw, of course, prefers Brown to Watts, though it is clear from his remarks that he is not entirely immune to Watts' idealized, beautiful world. Finally, he notes that Ibsen, the realist, developed out of Ibsen the idealist. Though he was to say so explicitly later, this is an early hint of his observation that the strong side of pre-Raphaelitism, its realistic side, grew out of its idealistic side. The problem of the two sides of the pre-Raphaelite coin confronts anyone who is interested in them. The problem troubled Shaw as well.

Occasionally Shaw permitted himself to admire paintings in a less realistic vein by another pre-Raphaelite artist whose work is heavily allegorical; these are the paintings of J. M. Strudwick, a painter less well known than Ford. Strudwick had been a studio assistant to Burne-Jones who is, after Rossetti, perhaps the most famous of the pre-Raphaelite painters. Strudwick's work very closely resembles that of Burne-Jones. Shaw begins his essay on Strudwick by a general criticism of tendencies in painting at the moment (1891). He criticizes the lack of imagination and genuine creativity in painting, noting that there are a number of remarkable draughtsmen at work, men who can deal with the minutest detail and reproduce it exactly, men who take endless pains, and produce not art but mere handicraft. What is lacking is mystical inspiration. Shaw finds the necessary element in Strudwick's painting; he specifically praises the fact that the pictures are "entirely invented," for Strudwick did not use models. Shaw goes on to praise "the charm of the architecture, the bits of landscape, the elaborately beautiful foliage, the ornamental accessories of all sorts which would distinguish them even in a gallery of early Italian painting."[8] In short, the work is pre-Raphaelite. Shaw has made a brief catalogue of the characteristics that define pre-Raphaelite painting in his mention of the architectural detail, the foliage, and the ornamental accessories.

Shaw had obviously admired the greatest of the pre-Raphaelites, Dante Gabriel Rossetti. He had seen two exhibitions of Rossetti's work in 1883, a year after the artist's death. In those two exhibitions he had seen over 200 paintings. Of them he had this to say three years later in 1886: "When Rossetti's work was first assembled at the Fine Arts Club, and, very soon afterwards, at the Academy, their wealth of color, poetic conception, and the fascination of the faces with which the canvases were crowded, dazzled all of those to whom Rossetti was new."[9] This is high praise, indeed, but he goes on, now referring to the 1886 exhibition of Rossetti's work at Christie's: "But our eyes are now used to the sun; and, at Christie's, Rossetti's want of thoroughness as a draughtsman, and the extent to which his favorite types of beauty at last begin to appear as mere Rossettian conventions, with impossible lips and mechanically designed eyebrows, came with something of a shock upon many who had previously fancied him almost flawless."[10]

Shaw's reference to Rossetti's "favorite types of beauty" may be slightly sour due to his encounter with one of the models who had been important in shaping Rossetti's ideal. She was Jane Burden Morris, the wife of William Morris whom Shaw met when he was visiting at Kelmscott. He has written of entering that "magical" house with its weirdly beautiful medieval-looking decorations. He was waiting in a hallway, a rather dark one apparently, when suddenly Jane Morris appeared. She was ten years older than she had been in Rossetti's paintings of her, but she was still very beautiful. She looked, he wrote, as though she were eight feet tall, almost as though she were a figure out of some Egyptian pharaoh's tomb. The impression was heightened by the fact that she was, says Shaw, "the silentest woman" he had ever met. She was like something out of the pre-Raphaelite dream. The only time she ever spoke to him, though he visited the house often, was at a time when she played a mean trick on him. Aware of his vegetarianism, she had been careful to see that he was served suitable food. One night she served an excellent pudding of which Shaw joyfully consumed two large portions. When he had finished his second plateful, she gleefully informed him that he had eaten a suet pudding. She must have seemed much less like a pre-Raphaelite dream to him after that incident.[11]

The Morris household had a considerable effect upon Shaw. As I noted, he said it was a "magical house ... Nothing in it was there because it was interesting or quaint or rare or hereditary ... everything that was necessary was clean and handsome: everything else was beautiful and beautifully presented."[12]

Morris' aesthetics and Shaw's socialism would seem to have little relationship to one another, and it was through politics that the two men came to be friends. Morris' aesthetic principles doubtlessly influenced Shaw, but it should be noted that Shaw had a considerable influence upon Morris' economic theories. Morris, in fact, actually said that "In economics, Shaw is my master."[13] William Gaunt in his important history of the Pre-Raphaelite Movement has made the following observation: "The echoes of Pre-Raphaelite Socialism may be found in the work of Mr. George Bernard Shaw who, in his interest in and encouragement of all who practise an art, and in his refusal to consider art as other than a means to a social end, may be considered (to that extent) a great living Pre-Raphaelite."[14] (That observation was made, incidentally, in 1942.) It is difficult to come to any clear understanding of what Mr. Gaunt means by pre-Raphaelite socialism, but I infer that he refers to the general belief held by all of the pre-Raphaelites that art is a central concern in the lives of men, and that through art it was possible to improve man's general lot. The pre-Raphaelites, partially due to the influence of Ruskin, were interested in contemporary movements aimed at bringing art into the lives of working men; Rossetti, for example, taught drawing for a time at the Working Man's College in London. But it is Morris who is the great political figure of the movement and it is Morris who must be seen as the only full-time pre-Raphaelite socialist.

Morris and Shaw did not agree on everything. Morris preferred to call himself a communist and was a firm believer in the Marxian concept of class warfare. He was strongly anti-parliamentarian and therefore did not approve of the legal and slower-moving methods of the Fabian socialists. It should be noted, though, that Shaw, writing in 1936 about Morris, noted ruefully that revolutions had accomplished more in a moment in Ireland and Russia than all of the years of Fabian agitation in Parliament had accomplished. Though Morris learned his economics from Shaw, it would seem that Shaw, in the late thirties at least, had come round to Morris' point of view in politics. The relationship of the two men was a pleasant and fruitful one for both of them, and it was through Morris that Shaw came into closest contact with "pure" pre-Raphaelitism.

I have been dealing with Shaw as an art critic and as a socialist, but the most interesting evidence of Shaw's debt to the pre-Raphaelites is in one of his most interesting plays, *Candida*. The Pre-Raphaelite Movement is, in fact, what the play is based on. By 1895 pre-Raphaelitism had come to an end, or perhaps I should say that it had undergone a metamorphosis into the aesthetic movement that dominates the end of the century. The idealism of the pre-Raphaelites had been changed into the finicky and precious idealism of art for art's sake, and what had started out as a reforming movement, had become an end in itself. In its way, it is sad, but Shaw was able to look at pre-Raphaelitism without the encrustations of aestheticism and to see in it a model for another kind of idealism, which went under the name of Christian socialism.

> In the autumn of 1894 I spent a few weeks in Florence, where I occupied myself with the religious art of the Middle Ages and its destruction by the Renascence. From a former visit to Italy on the same business I had hurried back to Birmingham to discharge my duties as musical critic at the Festival there. On that occasion a very remarkable collection of the works of our British "pre-Raphaelite" painters was on view. I looked at these, and then went into the Birmingham churches to see the windows of William Morris and Burne-Jones. On the whole, Birmingham was more hopeful than the Italian cities; for the art it had to shew me was the work of living men, whereas modern Italy had, as far as I could see, no more connection with Giotto than Port Said has with Ptolemy. Now I am no believer in the worth of any mere taste for art that cannot produce what it professes to appreciate. When my subsequent visit to Italy found me practising the playwright's craft, the time was ripe for a modern pre-Raphaelite play. Religion was alive again, coming back upon men, even upon clergymen, with such power that not the Church of England itself could keep it out ... .
>
> Now unity, however desirable in political agitations, is fatal to drama; for every drama must present a conflict. The end may be reconciliation or destruction; or, as in life itself, there may be no end; but the conflict is indispensable: no conflict, no drama. ... To distil the quintessential drama from pre-Raphaelitism, medieval or modern, it must be shewn at its best in conflict with the first broken, nervous, stumbling attempts to formulate its own revolt against itself as it develops into something higher. A coherent explanation of any such revolt, addressed intelligibly and prosaically to the intellect, can only come when the work is done, and indeed *done with*: that is to say, when the development, accomplished, admitted, and assimilated, is a story of yesterday. Long before any such understanding can be reached, the eyes of men begin to turn towards the distant light of the new age. Discernible at first only by the eyes of the man of genius, it must be focussed by him on the speculum of a work of art, and flashed back from that into the eyes of the common man. Nay,

> the artist himself has no other way of making himself conscious of the ray: it is by a blind instinct that he keeps on building up his masterpieces until their pinnacles catch the glint of the unrisen sun. ...
>
> Here, then, was the higher but vaguer and timider vision, the incoherent, mischievous, and even ridiculous unpracticalness, which offered me a dramatic antagonist for the clear, bold, sure, sensible, benevolent, salutarily shortsighted Christian Socialist idealism. I availed myself of it in Candida.[15]

It seems to me that this is one of Shaw's most important statements about the nature of artistic genius. Though he chose to write about Christian socialism specifically, he could see in it the problems inherent in pre-Raphaelitism itself. The "quintessential drama" of pre-Raphaelitism arose from its "own revolt against itself." The drama lies in its paradoxical belief in action coupled with an escape from the present; it lies too in its attempt to do away with the Philistine, because it may be said that some of the pre-Raphaelites became Philistines themselves. Millais is the saddest example of this; a child prodigy, a painter of enormous talent and one of the idealistic young founders of the PRB he came to see success in terms of his own income. The price a picture fetched could indicate its artistic merit. His career is an illustration of the problems inherent in the whole movement. Like James he could not see that success on a broad scale did not necessarily guarantee one a place in heaven. Millais came to be regarded with suspicion by all serious critics, yet Shaw remained sympathetic, just as he remained sympathetic to Morrell even though he coldly presented him with the horrible ordeal of seeing himself as a self-centred and unwittingly selfish man. Of Millais, when he had fallen from grace, Shaw said: "That his aims were of the highest when he was a pre-Raphaelite brother is never questioned; and the lamentation over him as a great genius is louder than ever now that he has stooped to accept a title. But the walls of the Grosvenor Gallery proclaim the Baronet the same man as the pre-Raphaelite; that is to say, a man possessed by an intense desire for color. ... All their landscapes tempt one to declare that no man has ever seen anything that Millais could not paint, although many men have painted things that he cannot see."[16] Like Millais, Morrell could do anything though he could not necessarily *see* everything. Millais, the pre-Raphaelite *manqué*, and Morrell, the Christian socialist were both men of talent and compassion who permitted their private comforts to blind them to the ideals of their respective -isms.

One may go further and not stretch a point too much to see all of *Candida* as an allegory of pre-Raphaelitism. Morrell represents the movement as a whole, idealistic, engaging, essentially evangelistic in spirit, yet unrealistic. Marchbanks may be seen as a personification of that other part of pre-Raphaelitism, which tried to escape from the mean realities of Victorian life. Some of the pre-Raphaelites did it by painting pictures about mythological and Biblical figures, placing their characters in picturesque medieval settings. As I said before, the models were contemporaries, and they were represented very realistically. Marchbanks was perfectly capable of seeing the reality of everyday life in the Morrell household when that reality was a matter of such things as human relationships and dependencies; he could not, however, bear to see the realities of onions which needed slicing or lamps which needed trimming. He would have taken Candida off to some pre-Raphaelite dream world. Burgess is obviously the Victorian Philistine, practical, tasteless, and suspicious of ideals.

That leaves us with Candida. If, as Shaw himself said, the play is a distillation of the quintessential drama of pre-Raphaelitism and shows that movement at the moment at which it "attempts to formulate its own revolt against itself as it develops into something higher," then Candida is the mysterious force that initiates that revolt just because she exists. Movements come and movements go and they develop from one thing into another and it is difficult to explain exactly why this happens. Perhaps it can be seen as the result of historical inevitability, to use a Marxian concept with which Shaw had certain sympathies. Candida, the great mother figure, is life itself. Because of her existence both the escapist, idealist Marchbanks and the idealistic self-styled realist Morrell are changed "into something higher."

Because pre-Raphaelitism was over and done with, Shaw could observe it and see it as the idea upon which he could build his domestic drama. As he noted, "a coherent explanation of any ... revolt can only come when the work is done. ... Long before any such understanding can be reached the eyes of men begin to turn towards the distant light of the new age." Shaw, because he was a genius, looked to the new age, one in which there was no real place for the self-divided -ism of the pre-Raphaelites. In their history he found the inspiration for art. In their rise and fall he found the pathos and comedy for *Candida*, his pre-Raphaelite play, and through his association directly or indirectly with their ideas at a crucial point of his career he found examples upon which he built the foundation of his own aesthetics.

NOTES

1 Archibald Henderson, *George Bernard Shaw: Man of the Century* (New York, 1956), pp. 175–6.
2 William Gaunt, *The Pre-Raphaelite Dream* (New York, 1966), p. 17. This book was originally published as *The Pre-Raphaelite Tragedy.*
3 Keith Andrews, *The Nazarenes* (Oxford, 1964), p. 80.
4 G. Bernard Shaw, "Madox Brown, Watts and Ibsen," *The Saturday Review,* 13 March 1897, p. 266.
5 Janet Dunbar, *Mrs. G.B.S.: A Portrait* (New York, 1963), p. 180.
6 Shaw, "Madox Brown, Watts and Ibsen," p. 266.
7 *Ibid.*
8 G. Bernard Shaw, "J. M. Strudwick," *Art Journal,* LIII (April 1891): 101.
9 Quoted by Henderson, p. 169, from the original source, *Our Corner,* May 1886.
10 *Ibid.*
11 George Bernard Shaw, "William Morris as I Knew Him," in vol. II of *William Morris: Artist, Writer, Socialist* (Oxford, 1936), pp. xxiv–xxv.
12 *Ibid.*, p. xx.
13 *Ibid.*
14 Gaunt, p.17.
15 George Bernard Shaw, *Plays Pleasant and Unpleasant,* Standard Edition (London, 1952), v–viii. This preface was first published in 1898.
16 Quoted in Henderson, p. 170.

CLIFFORD LEECH

Shaw and Shakespeare

Niagara-on-the-Lake is my second Shaw Festival, for over a period of years I made a habit of going to that Festival at Malvern in England which Sir Barry Jackson started in 1929. Of course, Shaw was alive then, and he was a friend of Sir Barry Jackson: naturally he came to see his own plays, and even the plays of other writers when they were performed along with his. When he had a new play ready, he let Malvern have it first. *The Apple Cart*, now happily to be revived here, was first acted at Warsaw in a Polish translation, but the first performance in English was the special attraction of the first Malvern Festival in 1929. I was an undergraduate then, and involved with things that prevented me from getting to Malvern. But the following year I had become a graduate, and was ready for the adventure of seeing Shaw's plays in a place specially dedicated to their performance. It was exciting enough to keep me going there regularly for some years. Shaw was the *genius loci*. He always had his seat in the front of the circle: he knew the plays were good, and he knew the performances were worthy of them. After all, the original cast of *The Apple Cart* included Edith Evans as Orinthia and Cedric Hardwicke as Magnus. Malvern, too, had a pleasant small theatre; and in its background were the Malvern hills, which had been part of English literature since the fourteenth century, when William Langland had made his Piers Plowman fall asleep there and dream out his vision of an England subject to Lady Meed – Riches, or Bribery, we could call her – but where an eccentric individual or two might spend his life striving to Do Well. It was appropriate to be reminded of Langland as we saw Shaw, for in our midst was another man who found his society misdirected and foolish, but did believe there were some men and women who refused to let Lady Meed blindfold them.

Not many miles eastward from Malvern there was another festival town, where Shakespeare was celebrated, and for some years the two festivals wore a pleasantly complementary air. Right in the centre of England, at Stratford, there was Shakespeare, the supreme dramatist in the English language; a little towards the west, appropriately a little nearer to Ireland, there was Shaw, the supreme English dramatist of the twentieth century. You can imagine that now in Ontario I feel curiously at home: here at Niagara is Shaw, over there to the west is Shakespeare at another Stratford. It is good to find, too, that the two dramatists have not exclusive rights in their festivals, as indeed was the case at Malvern all those years ago. This year we do have all Shaw at Niagara, but last year there was an O'Casey play, and I hope that is going to be a precedent to return to. Few things can help us to see the special quality of a man's writing more clearly than having his plays performed along with those of his contemporaries and predecessors and immediate successors. So I hope that Niagara will give us more O'Casey, and will do Synge and Pinero and Granville-Barker, and later writers too, in the same way as our own Stratford has given us Molière and Wycherley lately and will perhaps before long try Marlowe and Ben Jonson and Webster.

"I wonder if Shaw's plays will last," people used to ask when he was alive. So far, at least, they do not seem to lack staying-power. The professional theatre in England has found staple fare in him lately, confirming Ontario's judgment in having its Shaw Festival. Of this year's three plays here, the oldest is *Man and Superman*, first acted in 1903. It is worth while asking ourselves which other dramatists writing in English are still holding the stage from that time. A scrutiny of programs from the London theatre in the earliest years of this century would, of course, show us Shakespeare as well as Shaw, and one or two others whose work is still being acted. This year the Royal Court Theatre has revived Granville-Barker's *The Voysey Inheritance*, which was written during the years 1903–1905, and the National Theatre at the Old Vic has been playing with delightful zeal Pinero's *Trelawney of the "Wells,"* first acted in 1898. But now let us turn back the clock further, another sixty-three years from 1903. We arrive at 1840, and can then ask how many playwrights whose work was then on the stage were still being acted in London in 1903. The answer is simple: "Shakespeare, and perhaps Sheridan." No new dramatist of the years around 1840 was actively contributing to the "West End" theatre sixty-three years later. In the history of the theatre, sixty-three years is indeed a long time, and Shaw has lasted ten years longer than that: his earliest play, *Widowers' Houses*, was first acted in 1893. He has, in fact, "lasted" for nearly three-quarters of a century. That is quite a long run.

Shaw did not hesitate to point out the differences between him and Shakespeare. In writing about his own *Caesar and Cleopatra* in the Preface to *Three Plays for Puritans*, he did not claim he was a better playwright than Shakespeare, but he did claim that he had a better idea of what Julius Caesar was like than Shakespeare had. No one, he said, had learned to write better plays than Shakespeare, but we had become better historians, better social critics, better scientists, than the men of Shakespeare's time were, and an intellectually gifted playwright would reflect all this in his plays. Indeed, we may go a step further than this. Since the beginning of this century we have learned a good deal more about society and the universe than Shaw knew: as an old man, he fumbled in handling some of the new knowledge, and even *The Apple Cart*, the best of his later political plays, shows him at times uncertain. He is excellent about "Breakages, Ltd.," anticipating the powerful development of what we have come to call the principle of "planned obsolescence"; but he is merely sentimental in finding an active role in the state for his clever Magnus. Nothing ages so quickly as the political play that strives to be supremely up to date, for we must distinguish between that and the play that deals with the permanent problems that confront men when they are trying to find a way of living together. Shaw's touch is most assured when he is dramatizing the attempt to cope with those permanent problems, while seeing them in the light of recent historical events and in the light of the change in manners and in beliefs which he found in his world and which has shown a more or less steady development right up to the present moment. Not that Shaw liked any revolution that he was not able to think his own. He disliked Darwinism because it left little room for the individual will, either human or (in the shape of the Life Force) transcending the human; he patronized Marx; he loved to shock freethinkers by insisting on the importance of religion; he resented disorderly behaviour as ungentlemanly and unladylike and irresponsible. This, for example, was how he wrote in 1931 in the long concluding speech of *Too True to be Good*, a play recently on view again in London:

> Throw off the last rag of your bathing costume; and I shall not blench nor expect you to blush. You may even throw away the outer garments of your souls: the manners, the morals, the decencies. Swear; use dirty words; drink cocktails; kiss and caress and cuddle until girls who are like roses at eighteen are like battered demireps at twenty-two: in all these ways the bright young things of the victory have scandalized their dull old pre-war elders and left nobody but their bright young selves a penny the worse. But how are we to bear this dreadful new nakedness: the nakedness of the souls who until now have always disguised themselves from one another in beautiful impossible idealisms to enable them to bear one another's company. The iron lightning of war has burnt great rents in these angelic veils, just as it has smashed great holes in our cathedral roofs and torn great gashes in our hillsides. Our souls go in rags now; and the young are spying through the holes and getting glimpses of the reality that was hidden.

Shaw wrote his plays at a time when men's minds were losing defences they had long known, when science and war and social revolution were pressing hard. These plays belong to the world that Darwin and Marx did so much to shape, however much Shaw might indicate a personal preference for Nietzsche. He mirrored his age without much liking it; he loved pretending to be "up to date" in thought, but he was at his best when he was not preaching the Shavian gospel but seeing the way men and women were responding, in a modern context, to the pressure of perennial demands.

And he did it lightly. There is not tragedy in Shaw, for tragedy is the dramatization of human disaster, and Shaw never properly faced that. His Joan died at the stake, but he had to bring her back to life in an epilogue where it is suggested that at some time the world might be ready for her. His *Widowers' Houses* and his *Heartbreak House* show people defeated by the society they are helping, in a fashion, to keep going, but there is perhaps the implication that elsewhere there are people of more drive and vision who will contribute to a new order. So he is the stubborn optimist who exhibits the stupid present but promises us or our remote descendants a more enlightened time. That became difficult for him at the very end of his career, when he turned often to a defiant frivolity: I am thinking of such unhappy plays as *Geneva* and *In Good King Charles's Golden Days*. But in the time of his major work he showed, with shrewdness and wit, what it was like to face the job of living together when nothing was standing still. *Man and Superman* is, of course, full of illustrations of this. Roebuck Ramsden was a man of advanced thought long before John Tanner became one: he is horrified at what "advanced thought" has come to mean. Henry Straker is the new technologist, cheerfully accepting Tanner's condescension but with time on his side. Tanner himself is the man who knows that his society is blinkered and hypocritical, but he can't live outside it: he may dream of the Superman, but he becomes the husband of Ann Whitefield.

And Ann, ready to defy convention in order to make the marriage she wants, has nevertheless a compulsion to keep her cards well hidden: in her last desperate though successful bid she even swoons. It is significant that only the new man, Straker, quickly sees what she is after. We may note in relation to Ann how much her position differs from that of Helena in Shakespeare's *All's Well that Ends Well*, a play for which Shaw seems to have had a considerable regard. Helena loves the high-born Bertram, and sets out to marry him. He does not love her, and Helena must indeed be resourceful to compel his attachment and even to subdue him when, surely unlike Tanner, he deserts her immediately after the wedding ceremony. She plays many skilful tricks, but it is important that at two moments of crisis – the first when the wedding is contrived, the second when she converts Bertram into an obedient husband – she has to get the aid of the King of France. No king is going to help Shaw's Ann. She is wholly on her own, and she has the further disadvantage of having to behave, in public, like a perfect lady. Her basic problem is Helena's, but Helena had a king to help her, and Helena could get into her husband's bed when he thought he was sleeping with another woman. Ann and Helena are sisters, but the lapse of three centuries had changed the context of their problem. What Shaw does is to make us see the basically unchanging problem with the special variations characteristic of 1903.

It is noticeable that in *Misalliance*, only seven years later, Hypatia makes no secret of her wish to marry Percival. When he says he hasn't enough money, having been expensively brought up in a household which would make married life on a thousand pounds a year seem "degrading poverty" – adding "Besides, I'm rather young to marry. I'm only 28" – Hypatia simply says to her father: "Papa: buy the brute for me." Ann couldn't have said that, but the seven years between 1903 and 1910 had made a difference. Of course, we don't like Hypatia much, and neither does Shaw. He makes Percival indicate that he is willing to marry her, at a price, because he doesn't find her physically unattractive, and in any event one woman is as likely as another to make a tolerable wife. That is meant to put Hypatia in her place, but all she minds about is getting her way – as indeed she does. She is not clever, like Ann or Shakespeare's Helena: she merely uses her father's money to buy a husband as she has used it for acquiring everything else she has. The woman in *Misalliance* that Shaw really admires, of course, is Lina, who is much more attractive than Hypatia but objects to love-making being the one dominant concern in the English household she is visiting, who has a profession of her own which she makes plenty of money from, and who delights in risking her life. Shaw always liked people who made money and enjoyed risks: they were in the vanguard of his society, getting pleasure from the head-on encounter with the future. So he liked Undershaft the armaments manufacturer in *Major Barbara.* He had no great fondness for those who merely acquiesced and followed the fashion. For him, there were those who passed the time and those who made time go faster; there were the passengers, and those who insisted on driving an unreliable car on an ill-made road: his sympathy was always with those who ran to meet their destiny. He was at one with Ibsen in finding a deeper recklessness, a readier defiance, in some women than in most men. So he is with Ann in her search for the Superman's father, he is almost willing to condone Hypatia's exploitation of her father's money – for she, after all, is pushing beyond a normal limit.

If I have emphasized that Shaw was mirroring his time, showing – as Shakespeare put it – "the very age and body of the time his form and pressure," that of course does not mean that in 1910 expensively brought up young women were in the habit of saying to their fathers "buy the brute for me," or that English country houses of those years were likely to have an enchanting Polish acrobat drop in on them for the week-end. Shaw is a dramatist, and he knew better than most people that the theatre is a place where you don't reproduce actuality: you present an image of it, which means that you aim at the essence, not the everyday appearance of things. Every now and again one does make a really startling encounter (though the occasions get fewer as the years go by): the dramatist can and must use such experiences, and make them more obviously startling than they ever truly are. When Romeo first sees Juliet, we remember, his words are:

> O, she doth teach the torches to burn bright!
> It seems she hangs upon the cheek of night
> As a rich jewel in an Ethiop's ear –
> Beauty too rich for use, for earth too dear!

Even falling in love is not quite like that. Nor is Lina quite like anyone we shall meet outside a theatre. But Shaw and Shakespeare make us realize the more vividly what it has been like to be really startled by seeing someone marked by a special difference.

There are indeed many ways in which we can see Shakespeare and Shaw as fellow-craftsmen of the theatre. There is a common but mistaken belief that Shakespeare is a dramatist of action and Shaw a dramatist of argument. It was a belief that Shaw liked to encourage. He wanted us to see Shakespeare as, in general, the magician with a grand spectacle for us to be moved and dazzled by, while he himself was the man who made us think, who directed our attention towards the immediate necessity of getting on terms with his special brand of socialism. At the end of Act 1 of *Too True to be Good*, the one actor remaining on the stage addresses us with the words:

> The play is now virtually over; but the characters will discuss it at great length for two acts more. The exit doors are all in order. Goodnight.

And both *Man and Superman* and *Misalliance* end with a mockery of all the talking that has been going on. Nevertheless, in the famous Preface to *Three Plays for Puritans* he admitted that he was, as a craftsman, a traditional dramatist with all the old tricks:

> But my stories are the old stories; my characters are the familiar

> harlequin and columbine, clown and pantaloon (note the harlequin's leap in the third act of Caesar and Cleopatra); my stage tricks and suspenses and thrills and jests are the ones in vogue when I was a boy, by which time my grandfather was tired of them.

In the same Preface he said that each philosophic period could produce only one dramatist whose work supremely embodied it, and that Shakespeare provided that embodiment for the Elizabethan age as he himself did for the first half of the twentieth century. What he did not say was what philosophic outlook it was that Shakespeare gave embodiment to.

Now if Shaw uses old theatrical devices – and indeed he does, as with Lina in *Misalliance* and Ann's schemes and Tanner's flight in *Man and Superman* and the King's turning the tables on the politicians in *The Apple Cart*, only to have the tables turned on him by the American Ambassador – so is it also true that Shakespeare works with argument and debate, at times very much in Shaw's manner. It will be worth while, I think, to spend a few minutes with the early comedy *Love's Labour's Lost,* which is in some ways a rather mysterious play because we don't know exactly when it was written and many of us suspect that it was first performed, not in a public theatre, but before an audience of nobles and notables in a great house. It seems to contain a remarkable number of sly hints about current goings-on in high society, and in particular the philosophical preoccupations of Sir Walter Ralegh's circle seem to be referred to. For a very long time *Love's Labour's Lost* was forgotten by the theatre, but it has come back into notice through performances both in England and at our Canadian Stratford during the past few years. It is by no means all talk, for the courtship of a princess and her three ladies by a king and his three lords is carried out with delicate, dancelike movements; there is, too, some wooing in masquerade, and some fun at the expense of amateur theatricals. Moreover, the king and his lords write love-poems to their ladies, and the play concludes with the famous Spring and Winter songs that have got into all the anthologies. Because these various poems show a wide range in form and style, Shakespeare gives us here a small anthology of his own, representing and sometimes mocking the contemporary fashions in verse-making. Nevertheless, this is emphatically a debate-play, first about the rival claims of study and love on a young man's attention, and then about the relation between courtship and marriage.

When the play begins, we find ourselves in the kingdom of Navarre, a place very much in Englishmen's minds around 1590 because its king, Henry, was the leader of the Protestant cause in France. But the king in the play is not Henry: he is a fictitious king with the name Ferdinand. He has persuaded three friends among his lords – Biron, Longaville, and Dumain – to join with him in forming an academy in which they will give all their time to study for three years, eating sparely, sleeping little, and seeing no woman. Although Biron promises to come into the scheme, he protests it will not work, and indeed reminds the king that they will have to make an exception immediately because the king has forgotten that the Princess of France is just about to arrive on a state visit. So they compromise: the princess must be received, but she and her ladies will not be allowed to enter the palace; they must stay during their visit in a pavilion in the royal park. It is not surprising that the women take this rather ill and are ready to make the men suffer for it. But as soon as a meeting between the two sides comes about, all four men fall in love – conveniently, each with a different woman; most conveniently, the king with the princess. This is theatre, where patterns can be assembled with a neatness transcending but imaging the often annoying neatness of real-life patterns. It is, moreover, appropriate that Biron, the dominant figure among the lords, who had already shown himself sceptical of the king's plan, should love the dominant lady Rosaline. Soon we see him sending her a letter, surreptitiously and with a good deal of self-castigation. He is ashamed that he who has mocked at love in the past should now be its victim; and there is the point, too, that he cannot understand why he has fallen in love with this particular woman. He compares her to a piece of machinery that without continuous attention is always going wrong:

> A woman that is like a German clock,
> Still a-repairing, ever out of frame,
> And never going aright, being a watch,
> But being watch'd that it may still go right!

He does not think her beautiful, and is ready to believe she is unchaste:

> A whitely wanton with a velvet brow,
> With two pitch-balls stuck in her face for eyes;
> Ay and by heaven, one that will do the deed
> Though Argus were her eunuch and her guard.

Still, though she may not be worth loving, love her he does and will: he "will love, write, sigh, pray, sue, and groan."

But at least he does not long lack company in affliction. When we see him next, he is still rating himself for being in love, and still writing poetry about it. But then he hides himself as the king enters and confesses in soliloquy that he loves the princess, reading aloud the poem he has written to her. Then in turn he stands aside when Longaville enters with his confession in soliloquy and reads his poem. Then Dumain comes in the same plight, and Longaville, unseen, listens to him. The pattern of the scene is now reversed: Longaville comes forward and denounces Dumain for failure to live up to their joint undertaking; then the king appears and rebukes them both; then Biron in triumph rebukes all three. Rashly he proclaims his own constancy:

> I, that am honest; I, that hold it sin
> To break the vow I am engaged in;
> I am betray'd, by keeping company
> With moon-like men, men of inconstancy.
> When shall you see me write a thing in rhyme?

In a moment his triumph is ended, for the Clown of the play comes in and brings back Biron's letter to Rosaline, which had gone astray. So now every one of them has shown himself forsworn, and they are badly in need of regaining lost face.

That is what the resourceful Biron is able to help them to. He persuades them to accept the idea that their purpose of giving themselves to study was correct, but the means they were to adopt to effect this purpose were faulty. True wisdom was to be found, not in books, but in women's eyes. From there the spirits of a man are vitalized: he sees and hears better through being in love; it makes him more valiant, more ingenious, more gifted in music, more eloquent with words. So let them follow learning in the true academy:

> From women's eyes this doctrine I derive:
> They sparkle still the right Promethean fire;
> They are the books, the arts, the academes,
> That show, contain, and nourish all the world;
> Else none at all in aught proves excellent.

Of course, we need not believe any of this, but it does provide a way out for Biron and his friends. They can convince themselves they are not forsworn after all, yet Shakespeare shows how specious the argument is by having the men, in their new-won freedom from shame, planning their campaign against "these girls of France" with plenty of bawdy double meanings in their excited talk. Clearly Biron does not himself believe that you don't need a book if you have a woman to look at instead. It was two hundred years later that a romantic poet could urge his reader to "Let Nature be your teacher" and could assure him that

> One impulse from a vernal wood
> May teach you more of man,
> Of moral evil and of good,
> Than all the sages can.

Shakespeare did not expect us to take Biron like that, merely substituting "Woman" for "Nature." Even so, there is real debate here: an opposition does exist between the claims of love and learning, an opposition comparable to that presented in the

Hippolytus of Euripides, where the hero was destroyed because he neglected the worship of Aphrodite and gave all his devotion to Artemis. But Shakespeare is writing comedy, so the men do not stay long from Aphrodite and speciously persuade themselves that she is an all-embracing deity.

But that is by no means the end of the matter. The women have been affronted by their reception in Navarre, and they do not believe the professions of love they are offered. This, they think, is a new way of mocking them. The men do what they can, coming as masquers in Muscovite costumes and being chased away, and then coming again without disguise to declare themselves and to offer a pageant entertainment which is given by their retainers. That is another disaster, for Shakespeare the professional could make fun of amateurs who took on more than their skill allowed, as he did in another comedy of those years, *A Midsummer Night's Dream*. The lords try to recover face again by joining in the mocking of their own servants. So much so that the audience's sympathy veers to the unskilful performers, and the lords' standing is at its lowest. They would have done so much better, we think, if they had persevered with their books.

And suddenly masquerade and courtship are over for a time. A messenger from the French court arrives, bringing the news that the King of France, the princess's father, is dead. The ladies must go: the affairs of life and death stand in the way of the learning that was to come from looking into a woman's eyes. The men take it well. With seriousness now they urge their love, and seek for marriage. But the princess and her ladies cannot be won so quickly to take a different view of the men, who must show the truth of their devotion by a year of separation and penance. Now they must expect, not the sociable semi-rigour of the king's academy, but solitude and hard living indeed. The princess tells the king he must

> go with speed
> To some forlorn and naked hermitage,
> Remote from all the pleasures of the world;

There stay, until the twelve celestial signs
Have brought about the annual reckoning.
If this austere insociable life
Change not your offer made in heat of blood;
If frosts and fasts, hard lodging and thin weeds,
Nip not the gaudy blossoms of your love,
But that it bear this trial and last love;
Then at the expiration of the year,
Come challenge me.

Two of the ladies echo their princess, and for them and her we may feel that this is little but the imposition on the men of a knight's period of trial in his lady's service. We are in a conventional world of medieval romance, except that standing by is the messenger of death who silently gives an edge to what would otherwise seem trite and merely "literary." But Rosaline, in a passage that Shakespeare seems to have added some time after the play was first written, brings us fully away from pretence into the world of actuality. Biron is a witty man: he can laugh at himself, he can argue speciously, he can talk men into anything. So Rosaline raises the question of the full relevance to life of this wit. Let him go among the sick, the tormented, the dying, and see how laughter fits there. She lays down her terms thus:

Oft have I heard of you, my lord Berowne,
Before I saw you, and the world's large tongue
Proclaims you for a man replete with mocks;
Full of comparisons and wounding flouts,
Which you on all estates will execute
That lie within the mercy of your wit:
To weed this wormwood from your fruitful brain,
And there withal to win me, if you please,
Without the which I am not to be won,
You shall this twelve month term from day to day,
Visit the speechless sick, and still converse
With groaning wretches; and your task shall be,
With all the fierce endeavour of your wit
To enforce the pained impotent to smile.

Biron knows how hard that task is:

To move wild laughter in the throat of death?
It cannot be; it is impossible:
Mirth cannot move a soul in agony.

Shakespeare here raises the whole question of comic writing: is it possible to accept it only if we forget a substantial part of the total human situation, or is it possible to see the jest of things while at the same time seeing the terror that goes along with the jest? He probably believed that there was room for a jest in any extremity, but he knew that this was a hard doctrine for men to take. The ending of the play is not solemn, but it is serious: we are reminded of the cycle of the year in the famous songs of Spring and Winter. Spring is a time of flowers and music, but also of mocking and cuckoldry; Winter brings cold and bad roads, and coughs and red noses, and being shut in with the odours of hot food. Both these songs have "a merry note" in them, but they bring us up against common things. Courtship is over, and its relation to the general pattern of life is left unresolved. Shaw saw Ann Whitefield's tricks as a means used by the Life Force in pursuing its attempt to breed the Superman. Shakespeare merely poses the opposition of ceremonial wooing and common living, and leaves it at that. But this opposition is as much an opposition of ideas as we found in the earlier debate between love and books. The play's final contrast of Spring and Winter is to be linked with the earlier contrasts, and a hint is given that a total humanity must find room for both love and books, for both ceremony and the abandonment of ceremony. "It is not good to stay too long in the theatre," said Bacon. That is doubtless true, but it is no argument in favour of spending all one's time in the kitchen. The year has its rise and fall, and human life has a place for both study and love, for both elaborate courtship and common living.

The pattern is more elaborate than Shaw's, and the argument is more systematically worked out than in many of Shaw's plays. Often in a Preface Shaw tries to find a coherence that the following play hardly justifies. *Misalliance* is an engaging country-house play, with more diversity and more edge than its Noel Coward successor, *Hay Fever*, of some fifteen years later. But Shaw's Preface entitled "Parents and Children" would make the earnest reader, who had not yet got to the play, believe that he was going to see a dramatized discourse on the education of the young and on relations between the young and the old. That is indeed part of the play's concern, but not all that much. Lina and the Gunner don't fit into that pattern, any more than Orinthia fits into the thought pattern of *The Apple Cart*. And if the young people are hardly a credit to their bringing up and reveal a hardly satisfactory relation with their parents, we are not likely to blame it on the faults of the English educational system, numerous as those doubtless are. When *The Apple Cart* was first acted, I was told that the opening part of the dialogue, on the human attachment to ritual, was there because Shaw originally intended to write a whole play on the subject: then he got interested instead in the relation between kingship and electoral government, but could not bring himself to throw away what he had written at the beginning; so it stayed in. Still, I am not suggesting I should have preferred him to take it out: not only is it good fun, but Shaw's mind was commonly discursive, needing the random distraction to provide a stimulus for a renewal of sharp-eyed observation. We do prefer *Misalliance* to its Preface, I think, though he keeps to the point in the Preface and has a whole series of points in the play. I have heard the complaint about his dramatic dialogue: "He always drops the argument at the point where it gets difficult." There is some substance in that, for Shaw's mind worked best when he freely allowed himself to be distracted, when he did not set himself too rigorously to follow a thought through. That could be managed all right with *Pygmalion* or *Man and Superman*, because in neither of those plays has the governing idea an inherent complexity: make a barely articulate flower-girl into a gracious lady, and you may have a human being on your hands; set a young woman of spirit on the trail of an advanced-thinking egoist, and his egoism will crumble. But even in *Pygmalion* we have the delightful distraction of Eliza's father and in *Man and Superman* the not so exciting affairs of Violet and the Malones and the agreeable but by no means searching portrait of Henry Straker. Shakespeare in *Love's Labour's Lost* makes his very clowns, in their innocence and their pretences, contribute to his total argument. Shaw is content to let us be diverted in every sense. We should not complain: it is the way he must work, and he gives us plenty of reward. But in this respect, as in some others, he is a different dramatist from Shakespeare.

Yet I have tried to indicate that they are by no means polar opposites. One thing that Shaw loved to do was to get his characters sitting down and just putting before us their different views of the matter under discussion. *Misalliance* is in this respect a static play: a great deal of it consists in people making points against each other. And in *Getting Married* he staged a prolonged debate on a single issue: not that the speakers worked to a conclusion, for Shaw does that better through action, as in *Man and Superman* and in *Pygmalion*, than through talk. But he did love the cut-and-thrust of argument, and loved too the ways in which different personalities responded to a single theme. Shakespeare, too, on occasion did this. In the Second Part of *Henry IV* he gives us a strange kind of history play, one in which hardly any fighting takes place: when a battle seems imminent, Prince John of Lancaster talks the rebels out of it, and, when their forces are dispersed, he sends the leaders off to immediate execution. For the rest of the play, we are shown again and again the juxtaposition of characters representing opposing viewpoints: Falstaff and the Lord Chief Justice, Falstaff and the Prince, Falstaff and Shallow, the Prince and his father, Falstaff and the newly crowned Henry v. It is predominantly a duologue play, with the identities of the speakers changing. A few years after writing that, Shakespeare came to *Troilus and Cressida*, and then staged the kind of ensemble debate scene which Shaw delighted in and which we see in this year's festival in *Misalliance* and *The Apple Cart*. Shakespeare's play is about the war that the Greeks made against the Trojans in revenge for the carrying off of Helen. Quite early in the play we see the Greek leaders in council. The war is not going well for them, and they are meeting to decide why this is so and what can be done to improve matters. Really we are at a committee meeting, with Agamemnon, leader of the expedition, in the chair. We listen to the usual sort of committee talk, which underlines the gravity of the situation and the perplexity of the members, and then Ulysses politely asks to be allowed to make his contribution. He sketches an idea of the universe which was a commonplace for Shakespeare's contemporaries: in the nature of things there was harmony, in the great pattern of the Ptolemaic universe and in the societies that men lived in; but any disturbance of that harmony, caused by a movement of a celestial body out of its ordained path, or by a similar usurpation of place in the world below, could bring the whole pattern into disorder; the Greek army was thus being disturbed by Achilles' refusal to fight; because one great man went awry, all the rest became insubordinate; in the interest of victory, in the interest of universal harmony, Achilles must be made to accept the principle of subordination, must obey the will of Agamemnon. Ulysses convinces everyone present, and they decide that Achilles must bow to the disciplines of war. But it is no good talking in such terms to Achilles: he is not interested in universal harmony or in the victory of the Greek cause; his concern is only with his personal aggrandisement. So, when Ulysses goes to talk with Achilles, he uses a quite different line of argument. In his great speech beginning "Time hath, my lord, a wallet at his back/Wherein he puts alms for oblivion," he urges that the world we live in is one in which there is no order, in which each man strives to get advancement over others, and Achilles must see to it that his pre-eminence in the past is not forgotten through his inaction in the present. It is nothing to Ulysses that in his two speeches he presents totally opposed views of the world – in the one an idea of essential harmony disrupted by a single man's ambition, in the other an idea of essential chaos in which each man must trample down his rivals. He speaks differently, and with fitting eloquence, to two different audiences. Shakespeare does not say he is right on either occasion: we are merely offered, for our scrutiny, two opposing ideas.

Then we see a council in Troy, with Priam presiding. The question being debated is whether the Trojans should bring the war to an end by returning Helen to her husband or whether they are in honour bound to keep her and go on fighting. The best warrior among them, their chief hope in battle, is Hector. But he argues that Helen is not worth what they are spending on her in the shedding of blood. They argue about what "worth" or "value" means: is it simply the price that men arbitrarily attach to this or that, or has it some relation to an inherent property of the thing? Hector insists that man is not the single arbiter of value. But Troilus, who is in love, retorts with the plea that, if one has entered into a commitment, as for example in marriage, one does not give up that commitment because it has proved to be more costly than one expected. The whole council is made to realize the danger that lies ahead of their debate when Cassandra the prophetess, Priam's daughter, warns them of the destruction of the city that will surely follow if they keep Helen. Hector proceeds to argue, ineffectively, that they have no right to persist in their possession of Helen, for the law of Nature bids them return her to her owner, her husband Menelaus, and every well-ordered nation has endorsed this law of Nature. He is unable to maintain his stand against his brothers, however, and he indicates he will go along with them "In resolution to keep Helen still."

Here we see a sharp distinction between Shakespeare's debate and Shaw's. Shakespeare left all issues ultimately open; Shaw wanted his debates to end with the theatre audience being made to see where the truth lay. I have said that Shaw was an optimist. It would be wrong to label Shakespeare simply as a pessimist, but there is no doubt that he saw men as most frequently coming to most dubious conclusions. In the council in the Greek camp he showed Agamemnon and the rest accepting Ulysses' argument from an uncertain premise: who knows, Shakespeare implies the question, that the universe and human society were normally good and only abnormally ill? And he makes us doubt this more strongly when a little later he shows Ulysses speaking convincingly to Achilles on the universe as a chaos in which every man's hand is lifted against every other man. Similarly, in Troy the questions of "value" and "commitment" are never resolved. All that happens is that the war goes on: Achilles fights again, not because Ulysses has argued him into it, but because his "male-varlet" Patroclus has been killed by Hector; Hector himself is treacherously killed, and at the end of the play the fall of Troy is nearer. The use of argument has led to nothing: neither of Ulysses' speeches about the universe has made any man act differently, and in Troy the emotive claims of commitment subdue the arguments from value and law.

One might put it this way: Shaw believed in argument, but Shakespeare did not. Shaw felt he could influence the development of things in his time, Shakespeare knew that he could only show men acting and speaking as they are and that all history is already written. Not surprisingly, Shakespeare reached his highest level in tragedy, Shaw in argumentative comedy.

It is good argument and good comedy. It isn't wholly ours, for Shaw did not live long enough, or did not remain mentally alert long enough, to grasp some of the special characteristics of our age. That is why his most living plays today are about the things that do not substantially change, are not susceptible of reformation. Whatever our immediate circumstances, we shall recognize Ann Whitefield and John Tanner. Where Shaw leaves us merely uncomfortable is in his occasional trick of producing a rabbit out of a hat, like King Magnus, and attempting to pass it off as Minerva's owl. With Roebuck Ramsden the case is different: a professor often feels some kinship with him.

But, though he wanted the conclusion to be right, though he would like his characters to have learned something, Shaw rejoiced in the diversity of his characters and of their points of view. And I believe Shaw is right, and the common belief wrong, concerning his relations with his characters. "Shaw simply uses mouth-pieces," we have often been told. But in the Epistle Dedicatory to A. B. Walkley that he prefixed to the published version of *Man and Superman*, he maintained that the opinions of his characters were right "only from their several points of view." They were the dramatist's views only "for the dramatic moment." While he was writing, while he was imagining the play on the stage, he identified himself with Tanner and Ramsden and even Mendoza (at least when Mendoza appears as the Devil). He thinks from inside Magnus, he delights in the sense of multiple consciousness that the large cast of *Misalliance* allows him. Hence the Preface which he writes afterwards often takes on the appearance of a retraction, because now he is thinking singly, as Bernard Shaw, or rather perhaps as that Shaw-persona he so strenuously cultivated might be expected to think. Shaw is so much a man of the theatre that, when he abandons the splendid multiplicity of comic drama, he is in some measure still inside the theatre, delivering a monologue and now himself wearing costume and make-up.

There is a passage in Hermann Hesse's *Steppenwolf*, that strange novel first published in 1927, which may reinforce what I have just said and may also clarify the distinction I have tried to make between Shakespeare, who achieved fullest expression in tragedy, and Shaw, who was uniformly a writer of comedy despite his frequent concern with major human problems and his occasional references to profound suffering. In *Steppenwolf* it is argued that the tragic position is rare because it involves a break with society as it is: "The few who break free seek their reward in the unconditioned and go down in splendor. They wear the thorn crown and their number is small." But there are many others who recognize the wretchedness of the common pattern of life but cannot be free of it: "they have to share their beliefs in order to live." For them, however, there is a third way, distinct both from rejection and from acceptance. This is the way of Humour, which "has always something bourgeois in it, although the true bourgeois is incapable of understanding it." Its world is more inclusive than tragedy's, because it "brings every aspect of human existence within the rays of its prism." It avoids "the leap into the unknown" which tragedy demands, but it is at least the best of compromises. What Hesse says here seems particularly appropriate to the Shaw whom society came to feel affectionate about though it did not much understand him:

> To live in the world as though it were not the world, to respect the law and yet to stand above it, to have possessions as though "one possessed nothing," to renounce as though it were no renunciation, all these favorite and often formulated propositions of an exalted worldly wisdom, it is in the power of humor alone to make efficacious.*

Tragedy is an overt challenge to society, but Humour, in the sense in which Hesse uses the term, is indicative of the greater unease. It neither rejects nor capitulates. It is the Major Disguise – which will help us to understand why Shaw wrote plays.

* Quotations from *Steppenwolf* are from the revised version of Basil Creighton's translation of 1929 (New York, 1965), pp. 54–5.

MARTIN MEISEL

Shaw and Revolution: The Politics of the Plays

My subject is the relation between Shaw's plays and his politics. I am not the first to be struck by a discrepancy between them more interesting than bland congruence or mere irrelevance. Shaw's playwriting was always relevant to his politics; but there were apparent contradictions between the one and the other for nearly three decades, starting with those earliest plays, which Shaw himself describes as deliberately propagandist, and lasting through the First World War.*

The discrepancy shows itself in an area I will loosely call "strategy." Shaw's politics – his Fabianism – had a strategy for achieving certain desirable social ends. Indeed, a common attack upon Fabianism was to charge that it was all strategy. His plays, like all plays, are designed to engage and manage an audience by creating and organizing a flow of response. They are, in other words, strategies for achieving certain aesthetic ends. Shaw's over-all dramatic strategy, however, was also directed towards creating a residual impact; that is, his plays are not designed merely to stimulate the audience for two hours or even to purge it of stresses in some Aristotelian fashion, leaving

* Others who have been interested in the discrepancy include E. Strauss, *Bernard Shaw: Art and Socialism* (London, 1942), and Alick West, *George Bernard Shaw: A Good Man Fallen Among Fabians* (New York, 1950). In the introduction to his *Bernard Shaw, 1856–1950*, amended ed. (New York, 1957), a work of many excellences, Eric Bentley comments ironically on "what [Shaw] is most famous for among the critical – Contradictions," and gives as his own finding, "Both/And: such is the Shavian inclusiveness" (pp. xix, xxii).

its members essentially unchanged. Rather they are designed to culminate in a state of feeling, often including uneasiness and unresolved stress, that will effect a permanent change in consciousness bearing on social change. With such residual impact, the plays as organizations of response are better understood as rhetorical, aimed at persuasion. But between what they seem to persuade to and the Fabian strategies aimed at social change there is an apparent discrepancy.

The strategies and opinions of the Fabian Society changed and developed, as did its individual members; but "Fabianism" as a word and an idea took on a distinctive character in the late eighties, just in the interval of Shaw's movement from fiction to the theatre. Fabianism came to mean evolution as opposed to revolution; gradualism as opposed to catastrophism; the achievement of socialism through constitutional and parliamentary means (initially through the "permeation" of existing political parties and local government); collaboration with all progressive and meliorist forces (or "practical socialism" as opposed to purist ideological concern); and, of course, middle-class intellectualism as opposed to Marxist proletarianism. The Fabians defined themselves in relation to the more Marxist and revolutionary Social Democratic Federation on the one side and the shifting groups of left or communistic anarchists on the other. Shaw reduced the strategy of the socialist groups from which the Fabians diverged to the following terms in what should have been his dotage:

> All ... had the same policy and program. They were to preach the Marxist description and explanation of the Capitalist system to popular audiences. These, on being convinced, would join the little society to which the preacher belonged, and subscribe a penny a week to it. They would abandon and abolish all rival proletarian combinations. When the pence and the membership had accumulated sufficiently, and recruited and united the "proletarians of all lands," Capitalism would be overwhelmed, and Communism established in its place within twenty-four hours or so.[1]

The Fabian alternative was "permeation" – that is, it "pressed its members to join every other association to which its members could gain admission, and infect it with constitutional Socialism" – and a propaganda deliberately aimed at the educated middle class.

It is important to register two points here. First, Shaw was not simply affected by Fabian socialism: he was one of its prime shapers, more responsible for the character and cohesion of the movement, its doctrine as well as its style, than any other individual, with the inevitable exception of Sidney Webb. Lenin's famous phrase, "a good man fallen among Fabians," is misleading. Shaw tended to dominate the meetings as Webb did the committee work; it was he who drafted the important policy statements; and he was the only Fabian to contribute two essays to the famous volume of 1889, *Fabian Essays in Socialism*, including the crucial essay on "The Transition to Social Democracy." Fabian policy for many years was Shavian policy. The other point is that while revolution can mean many things, *all* socialist sects understood and desired it as a general, all-embracing transformation of society, as opposed to a merely negative cancellation of the *status quo*. Revolution can point to means as well as ends, however, and the substitution of a new social order for the *status quo* can be imagined as convulsive and violent or gradual and peaceful, and, if peaceful, effected through either coercion or persuasion. Whether violence was a necessary or indeed even a possible means to the end of socialist revolution provided much of the argument between the Fabians and their fellow socialists. (All sides could point to the lessons of the Paris Commune.) Still, the alpha and omega of Fabianism remained revolutionary; that is, it began in an overwhelming repudiation of things as they are, and its ultimate object was a radical and comprehensive transformation of society. From the vantage of 1916, Edward Pease, the moderate, not to say prissy, secretary of the Society and member from the earliest days, wrote about its beginnings in terms worth quoting at length if only because they are so very pertinent to our own current scene:

> The political parties ... offered very little attraction to the young men of the early eighties, who, viewing our social system with the fresh eyes of youth, saw its cruelties and its absurdities and judged them, not as older men, by comparison with the worse cruelties and greater absurdities of earlier days, but by the standard of common fairness and common sense, as set out in the lessons they had learned in their schools, their universities, and their churches.
>
> It is nowadays not easy to recollect how wide was the intellectual gulf which separated the young generation of that period from their parents. ... Our parents, who read neither Spencer nor Huxley, lived in an intellectual world which bore no relation to our own; and cut adrift as we were from the intellectual moorings of our upbringings, recognising, as we did, that the older men were useless as guides in religion, in science, in philosophy because they knew not evolution, we also felt instinctively that we could accept nothing on trust from those who still believed that the early chapters of Genesis accurately described the origin of the universe, and that we had to discover somewhere for ourselves what were the true principles of the then recently invented science of sociology.[2]

By labouring the notion that the origins and ends of Fabianism were revolutionary, I do not wish to ignore what lies between, its living or "objective" character, especially as experienced by its radical contemporaries whom it struck as profoundly unrevolutionary. A clue to what brought about this anomaly lies in Pease's account. Evolutionary doctrine, which he makes the great divide, ran counter to that sense of revolutionary alienation, that discontinuity of the generations, energizing the Fabians in the first place. Webb's *Fabian Essay* on the historic basis of socialism, for example, is saturated with a post-Darwinian use of the idea of the "social organism." He repudiates the notion of some ideal static Utopia as a socialist objective. And he declares, "The necessity of the constant growth and development of the social organism has become axiomatic. No philosopher now looks for anything but the gradual evolution of the new order from the old, without breach of continuity or abrupt change of the entire social tissue at any point during the process. ... history shews us no example of the sudden substitution of Utopian and revolutionary romance."[3] Webb, incidentally, does not conceive himself to be dealing only in metaphor or analogy; rather he sees social evolution as the present path of the whole evolution of life. As strategy, or process, or means to an end – that of social justice and a better world – evolution displaces revolution. But practically and even ideologically the process seems to become the end itself.

Nevertheless, as Shaw tells us in his history of the first years of the Fabian Society, when he joined in 1884 it was as "insurrectionary" and anarchistic as any rival group, and Shaw very nearly joined the Democratic (later Social Democratic) Federation instead.[4] Even after the Society had defined its policy as permeative, piecemeal, and evolutionary, and Shaw had taken to stigmatizing his revolutionary opponents as catastrophists (a term borrowed from discredited positions in geological and evolutionary controversy), his ambivalence about the strategy he helped to create would occasionally appear in the perorations of his political writings and speeches. In "The Transition to Social Democracy," in which he argues the impossibility of a "catastrophic" transition if only because the modern economic and industrial order is so complex, Shaw ends by saying:

> Let me, in conclusion, disavow all admiration for this inevitable, but sordid, slow, reluctant, cowardly path to justice. I venture to claim your respect for those enthusiasts who still refuse to believe that millions of their fellow creatures must be left to sweat and suffer in hopeless toil and degradation, whilst parliaments and vestries grudgingly muddle and grope towards paltry instalments of betterment. The right is so clear, the wrong so intolerable, the gospel so convincing, that it seems to them that it *must* be possible to enlist the whole body of workers – soldiers, policemen, and all – under the banner of brotherhood and equality; and at one great stroke to set Justice on her rightful throne. Unfortunately, such an army of light is no more to be gathered from the human product of nineteenth century civilization than grapes are to be gathered from thistles. But if we feel glad of that impossibility; if we feel relieved that the change

is to be slow enough to avert personal risk to ourselves; if we feel anything less than acute disappointment and bitter humiliation at the discovery that there is yet between us and the promised land a wilderness in which many must perish miserably of want and despair: then I submit to you that our institutions have corrupted us to the most dastardly degree of selfishness. ...[5]

I give this particular passage at length because it is the most frequently cited by writers who wish to show that in Shaw there was also the storm. Be that as it may, there is no uncertainty here as to the realism and indeed necessity of the Fabian course to social justice. It is true that the last word of the address declares that the catastrophist's program "still remains as the only finally possible alternative to the Social Democratic program which I have sketched today"; but the logic of the whole *including* the impassioned peroration demonstrates the impossibility of achieving the ends desired by all through a sudden and convulsive change, through a classical revolution.*

The truth is that the vast bulk of Shaw's political writing and speaking from about 1885 to World War I argued or presupposed the necessity of an evolutionary as opposed to a catastrophic transition to socialism, whereas his plays, beginning with the one he started in 1884 and finished in 1892, did nothing of the sort. In 1888, a month before he delivered "The Transition to Social Democracy" as a lecture to the Economics Section of

* Both West and Strauss make much of the passage. There is even more fire in the peroration of *The Fabian Society: What It Has Done*, etc., originally delivered to a Conference of the London and Provincial branches: "Whilst our backers at the polls are counted by tens, we must continue to crawl and drudge and lecture as best we can. When they are counted by hundreds we can permeate and trim and compromise. When they rise to tens of thousands we shall take the field as an independent party. Give us hundreds of thousands, as you can if you try hard enough, and we will ride the whirlwind and direct the storm" (p. 160). The vigour of the final cadence, very appropriate to the occasion, is nevertheless yoked to (in the language of the day) a "practical" or "possibilist" political programme, socialism through the ballot box. A. M. McBriar, the foremost modern historian of Fabianism, describes Shaw in this period as holding together a divided Fabian Society "with belligerent words and moderate recommendations" (*Fabian Socialism and English Politics*, 1884–1918 (Cambridge, 1966), p. 246).

the British Association, he amused and annoyed his fellow socialists with a sketch in the socialist magazine *To-Day*, radically different in mood and manner but arguing through a fiction the same point of view. The sketch may be regarded as a half-way house between the two modes of expression, discursive and dramatic.* "My Friend Fitzthunder, the Unpractical Socialist," by "Redbarn Wash" is the exasperated character-sketch of a catastrophist and "Impossibilist" – one who rejects available political and parliamentary avenues as contaminating – by a young socialist who was once his admirer. Fitzthunder insists on socialism (defined as "placing in the hands of the people the land, capital and industrial organization of the country") at once and entire, and dismisses anything less, including especially democratic political reform, as "a mere palliative." The result is the exclusion of socialists from most progressive enterprises, and effective support of the *status quo*. Of Fitzthunder's excuse for this anomaly, Wash writes, "Usually he takes a hint from Mr. Micawber, and explains that he is collecting himself for a spring. The workers, he says, are not yet organized for revolution – and Fitzthunder insists on revolution. The achievement of Socialism without it would be to him as flat as a pantomime without a transformation scene. ..." Wash connects Fitzthunder's revolutionary heroics with "the refuse of sensational novels, epic poems, and Italian opera." He connects it also (as in his essay of 1896, "The Illusions of Socialism") with popular religion, a tendency "to conceive the evolution of Socialism as a miraculous catastrophe, with alarums, excursions, and red fire."[6] In the next issue of *To-Day* there appeared "Fitzthunder on Himself – A Defence," by Robespierre Marat Fitzthunder, also Shaw.[7] The persona this time is pious, dull, humourless, passionate, and self-righteous. He charges Wash with holding up to the "scorn and ridicule of the common foe" socialism's great leaders including H. M. Hyndman (leader of the S.D.F.) and William Morris,

* For Shaw's tendency to personify ideas and points of view in his discursive prose, see Richard Ohmann's study, *Shaw: The Style and the Man* (Middletown, 1962).

whose pronouncements Fitzthunder has been merely echoing. The effect, of course, is to embellish the point of the first sketch, to rub in the irony through a further irony.

Despite Fitzthunder's outrageous stupidity, there is a hint of some ambivalence in Shaw's assumption of both personae, a hint made broad in the beginning of Wash's last paragraph, where he apologizes for having to assassinate "my poor friend – my other self, and the best fellow in the world." Wash's objection is specifically "to have anything to do with him in his public capacity," an objection shared by others "who are among the ablest Socialists we have got."[8] Clearly, Shaw's "ambivalence," his own Fitzthunderism, was not likely to break out unawares. (He subjects such ambivalence to a lucid and sustained analysis in his chief essay on the psychology of the socialist, "The Illusions of Socialism," to be discussed further on.) Moreover, his objection to Fitzthunder, to having anything to do with him "in his public capacity," would seem to cover the persuasive plays that Shaw soon began writing, plays that were as public as he could make them and the unregenerate state of the theatre would allow. Consequently, I am not content to take what seem to be important elements of catastrophism and impossibilism in the plays as the "real" Shaw, or even as the suppressed Shaw breaking out in the irresponsible dreamwork of art as personal expression. If it is true that, although he is in remarkably little evidence in Shaw's political writings and speeches except as straw man or scarecrow, Fitzthunder's spirit seems to hover over the ultimate statement of some of the plays, then one must assume that he is there with the full consciousness of the author and to serve some strategic intent.

PLAYS AND AUDIENCES: FIRST STRATEGY

When Shaw later decided to call his first three plays "Unpleasant Plays," he was advertising in that title a strategy that included audience revulsion, an assault on audience sensibilities. The name no longer strikes us as paradoxical, since aggression against the audience is a convention of the modern theatre, but it was not of the theatre of the nineties. By Shaw's own account of these plays, their strategy was, while entertaining the audience, to make its members uncomfortable, aware of their complicity in the social crime. "The didactic object of my play," he wrote of *Widowers' Houses*, soon after its performance in 1892, "is to bring conviction of sin."[9]

Widowers' Houses, however, was an experiment, and the "didactic object" was initially complicated by another. According to Shaw, the play was also designed "to induce people to vote on the Progressive side at the next County Council election in London."[10] Although it demonstrates with the logic of a paradigm the complicity of the *whole* of society in slum landlordism, the play suggests that the County Council and the vestries could at least alleviate the worst of the abuses; could provide, in other words, one of those "paltry instalments of betterment." But this strategy conflicts with others in the play, and is – as Shaw seems to have realized – about as adequate to the scale of the demonstration of universal complicity as a proposal by the Duke of Albany to endow public storm shelters might be at the end of *King Lear*. Consequently when Shaw revised *Widowers' Houses* he markedly reduced the availability of such easy ways out for the entangled conscience; and no such piecemeal alleviation is suggested in either of the other two plays he called "unpleasant." In *Widowers' Houses* (in its final version), municipal reform and the fact that (as the landlord says) "We live in a progressive age" simply provides the opportunity for a financial killing through fraudulent compensation.

The emotional logic of the play proceeds through the demonstration of the integrity of the social fabric in which all are implicated – slum-dwellers, rentiers, and aristocrats, as well as landlords and rent collectors – and its necessary corollary is the futility of piecemeal tinkering and private action. When the dazed young protagonist asks, "Do you mean to say that I am just as bad as you are?" the slum landlord rejoins, "If ... you mean that you are just as powerless to alter the state of society, then you are unfortunately quite right." And Harry Trench is forthwith "*morally beggared.*" To bring "conviction of sin" effectively the logic of the play can admit no relief in "paltry measures," nor can it allow an escape for the spectator through blaming individual villainy. Revulsion is deliberately displaced from the parts to the whole, from the slumlord (or the prostitute) to the System; and the issue for the audience, as for its once-innocent surrogate, becomes what it was for Fitzthunder: All or Nothing.

The end of the play narrows and enforces a "residual impact." The alternatives offered or implied are in fact not two but three: to acquiesce in the reality of one's complicity and make the best of it; to flee into private worlds of feeling and imagination; or to will the overthrow of the whole. The end of the play illustrates the first alternative in all its disagreeableness, and explodes the second alternative as illusory, leaving the third as the unstated terminus of the emotional dialectic. Trench accepts the first alternative: he "stands in" at the end with the others, to make the best of his threatened resources. His action undermines the second alternative, subjective withdrawal and private fulfillment; for the romance of the play, Trench's alliance with the slumlord's daughter, is now consummated (whether Trench admits it or not) only as part of the compact between land, capital, and enterprise. The audience is left, then, with the third unstated alternative: a revulsion from the whole in which all are so thoroughly implicated that the only release can be in the will to transform the whole.

The constituent nature of that audience ought not to be left vague, since an artistic strategy that is ultimately persuasive must take account of special qualities; and, moreover, Shaw in every public performance played directly to what he thought to be the special character of his audience. Shaw wrote his first three plays for an essentially coterie audience, self-consciously "advanced" and intellectual, though middle class in its habits of thought and standards of life; the same people in other words who provided the membership of the Fabians, except less philistine and more art-oriented than the Fabians, and as a group uncommitted to socialism. In February 1885 – a time when some Fabians still contemplated revolutionary means – Shaw delivered a lecture called "Proprietors and Slaves" to a non-socialist middle-class audience with similar qualities of high-mindedness and a relative openness to advanced thought. He addresses his audience from "the Liberal and Social Union" as "a body of ladies and gentlemen of more than ordinary culture"; and accuses them (and himself) from a socialist point of view of being "cannibals of the most dangerous description."* "Bad as we are," Shaw continues, "I believe that, if we all understood how we are living, and what we are doing daily, we should make a revolution before the end of the week. But ... we do not know, and ... many of us, foreseeing unpleasant revelations, do not want to know" (p. 5).

But while confronting the audience with some of these "unpleasant" truths, the lecture proceeds to use revolution chiefly as a threat. Revolutionary violence may be generated by the despair of the poor, or (more likely) by the proprietors' attempts at coercion and intimidation. For that reason Shaw's audience – presented to themselves as a temperate, responsible "middle class" – should educate themselves in socialism, "to fortify whatever is just in Socialism, and to crush whatever is dangerous in it." They especially are capable of disinterestedly "interfering on behalf of justice," and the presence of large numbers of the middle class in a socialist movement would "raise the Socialists above the danger of Coercion." Moreover, "When a Revolution approaches, those who are within the Revolutionary party can do something to avert bloodshed: those who hold aloof can only provoke it. A party informed at all points by men of gentle

* In Bernard Shaw, *Platform and Pulpit*, ed. Dan H. Laurence (New York, 1961), p. 1. The Liberal Social Union (*sic*) is described as one of several "organizations of middle class agnostics" with an ethical-religious tendency in Paul Thompson's *Socialists, Liberals and Labour: The Struggle for London, 1885–1914* (London, 1967), p. 33.

habits and trained reasoning powers may achieve a complete Revolution without a single act of violence" (p. 11). Making "unpleasant revelations" and demonstrating complicity was in the essential strategy of *Widowers' Houses* and the other Unpleasant Plays; but beyond disposing an audience to "make a revolution before the end of the week" *Widowers' Houses* does not go. Revolution as whole-cloth transformation is the end to which the argument of the play leads; in the speech, violent revolution is a means of persuasion to rational change, although the unconverted audiences for play and speech are in many essential respects of class and culture the same. The theatre setting makes a difference, of course. Accordingly, the speech seems to subordinate the logic of feeling to rational and prudential considerations, whereas the play makes rational argument part of the structure of feeling. The play has its own firm logic. The most rational characters, however, those with the plausible arguments, serve to dispel a number of flattering illusions, but are there in the end to have their reason rejected, to energize the reaction towards an alternative. *Widowers' Houses* aims to prepare and capture the will, not the reason; and (as we shall see) the will is conceived as revolutionary and catastrophic in its changes, concerned with ends rather than means, and with justice rather than prudence.

The better-known *Mrs. Warren's Profession* has a very similar strategy. It is a demonstration, using an audience surrogate, of general complicity in what was conceived to be the social crime *par excellence*, prostitution. What is demonstrated is not only the inextricable involvement of all in prostitution, but prostitution's inextricable involvement in the whole economic and social fabric. Prostitution works as a metaphor for capitalist arrangements that leave no innocence untainted; but the demonstration is literal and logical as well as analogical. Since real prostitution is so inextricably involved with the entire social fabric, piecemeal reformism on this favourite ground is invalidated as a solution; only total transformation will serve.

Mrs. Warren's Profession makes a particular point of the futility and inadequacy of the second alternative in the series described above, escape into the realm of the private emotions and the imagination. Poetry, art, and "love's young dream" are thoroughly undermined in the romantic illusionist Praed, and through the ironic context that prostitution supplies for an innocent young love. But this strategy of disillusionment, promoting "realism," is not the whole strategic use of the idea of subjective fulfilment. In the end Vivie Warren, Mrs. Warren's daughter and Trench's counterpart, is formidable but seared and maimed in her horror of love and all that involves feeling, her now resolute philistinism, her plunge into work – actuarial and statistical – which as yet has no ethical object. Her strength is offered as a model; but her spiritual crippling, more than anything, creates that residual sense of unpleasantness, that sense of the inadequacy of the available alternatives short of the unnamed one, general revolutionary transformation.

The Philanderer forecloses the alternative of escape into private fulfilment and anarchistic individualism even more directly. It puts on the stage the Independent Theater audience itself, as a coterie of liberated intellect and advanced sensibility. The play, set among Ibsenites and Shavians, demonstrates the inadequacy of both conventional sexual arrangements and individual attempts to transcend them. Merely to be liberated and free to follow one's bent and rationalize it produces as much unhappiness and absurdity as the prevailing system. Salvation will not come through an expanded individualistic liberalism and the pursuit of private fulfilment any more than through a piecemeal reform and refinement of the *status quo*.

ALTERNATIVE STRATEGIES

That the plays I have been discussing, and am chiefly concerned with, point implicitly to revolution as an end is not in itself surprising or anti-Fabian. What seems anti-Fabian is that the Unpleasant Plays (and some of Shaw's Edwardian "Discussion Plays," such as *Getting Married*) should, as part of their strategy, demonstrate the futility of gradualism or piecemeal reform in insisting on the integrity of all social and economic arrangements. Shaw's Pleasant Plays and Plays for Puritans (which succeeded the Unpleasant Plays chronologically) do not follow this strategy, although they have a relation to it and also have their own discrepancies with Fabianism. Their focus is the private imagination of the audience, truth and illusion, the interplay between private and public ideals. All in the end present a radical criticism of the theoretical value structure, the sustaining ideals, of contemporary – that is, bourgeois – society. This is nearly self-evident: *Arms and the Man* undermines ideals of military glory and romantic love; *You Never Can Tell*, liberal rationalism and individualism as they flowered in Mill and Herbert Spencer; *Candida*, domesticity in its philistine and idealist versions; *The Devil's Disciple*, virtue, romantic love, and gentility; *Captain Brassbound*, justice and the romance of empire; *Caesar and Cleopatra*, romantic heroism and political liberalism.* What is remarkable and discrepant is that, whereas many Fabians were critical of many aspects of contemporary middle-class values and ideals, the Fabian Society as a self-consciously middle-class grouping sought an extension of these values and ideals, their realization not in one class but in all. The Fabians insisted on not merely the suffering but the demoralization of the poor under capitalism, and concluded that, whereas violence might come from the poor, socialism would not. If the poor were indeed the repository of virtue – Shaw

* *Captain Brassbound* would seem to illustrate the futility of violent action (stigmatized as melodramatic revenge) as a means of overturning and achieving a genuine alternative to present institutions (injustice in the robes of Justice). *The Devil's Disciple*, however, demonstrates the efficacy of violent action against coercive authority when such action is organized and directed with an intelligent grasp of ends. The difference is interesting, but these aspects seem less important to me in the rhetorical strategy of the plays than the attack on sustaining bourgeois ideals.

often argued – any effort to tamper with their condition should be strenuously put down.[11] Their virtues in a transformed society however, where of course they would not be The Poor, would be middle-class virtues: sobriety, respectability, responsibility, a sense of fair play, even class solidarity. As Snobby Price says in *Major Barbara*, "In a proper state of society I am sober, industrious and honest; in Rome, so to speak, I do as the Romans do." Fabian strategy made large use of this prospect of universal respectability, in making its respectable recruits. As Shaw wrote in a 1908 preface to *Fabian Essays*, when the Society turned its back to the barricades, "We set ourselves two definite tasks: first, to provide a parliamentary program for a Prime Minister converted to Socialism as Peel was converted to Free Trade; and second, to make it as easy and matter-of-course for the ordinary respectable Englishman to be a Socialist as to be a Liberal or a Conservative."*

* *Essays in Fabian Socialism*, p. 292. The Fabian view of the part to be played by the working classes in bringing about socialism was not as consistently non-Marxist as is often assumed. In 1892, in the light of considerable gains being made by the "New Unionism" and the reluctance of the Liberals to make room for more progressive candidates in the upcoming election, the Society issued Shaw's *Fabian Election Manifesto* as Tract 40. With a great deal of hedging on immediate tactics, the manifesto argues the need for a "genuine Working Class party" (p. 8) and the immediate desirability of working-class candidates on grounds and with a rhetoric that assume the class conflict. Aimed at the working classes, it argues against their prejudice for middle-class spokesmen, "ambitious young lawyers and journalists who have no other way of compelling the political parties to recognize their talents" (pp. 12–13), and holds up as a model the propertied classes, who organize themselves behind routine class representatives as a matter of course. The manifesto is intended as a goad to political activity, and neither flatters nor attempts to be fair to those it addresses: "Slavery is popular in England provided the wages are regular: Socialism is only applauded when its propagandists give free lectures, distribute free literature, and do other people's political drudgery for nothing. The average British working man is a political pauper: he will neither do his own political work, nor pay anyone else to do it for him; and the result is that he is also an economic pauper, the mere tool and drudge of a class which leaves no stone unturned, and spares no expense, to secure the control of the State for itself" (p. 15). On the other hand, the Tract makes any

The problem arose, as Shaw was to argue critically, when middle-class values were embodied in ideals and ideals took precedence over reality. The reality was that the system of social theft was destructive of middle-class values and virtues in the life of the masses, and indeed in the life of society as a whole. And the confusion of those values with the institutions that purported to embody them – of Justice with the Judge's trappings, of sociability with marriage and the family – and the substitution of the Ideal for the deplorable reality in middle-class thought and imagination, prevented rather than assisted remedial transformation. The strategy of the Pleasant Plays, then, was to revolutionize the mind and imagination by disintegrating conventional ideals, and making attractive an unilluded imaginative realism; that of the Plays for Puritans was to detach the sustaining ideals and protective illusions of the *status quo* from a core of genuine values.

A dominant dramatic and thematic element in the Plays for Puritans is conversion. From the moments of disillusioning illumination, which educate the protagonists of the Unpleasant and Pleasant Plays, to the idea of conversion is only a step, but a clarifying step; for conversion is, in effect, a revolution of the

sort of progress seem wholly unlikely without organized working-class pressure.

In contrast, the 1896 *Report on Fabian Policy* (Tract 70, also Shaw's handiwork and the *locus classicus* of Fabian principles) appeared after the apparent dead failure of the new Independent Labour Party to made headway with the unions or at the polls. The section called "Fabians and the Middle Class" says in part: "In view of the fact that the Socialist movement has been hitherto inspired, instructed, and led by members of the middle class or 'bourgeoisie,' the Fabian Society, though not at all surprised to find these middle class leaders attacking with much bitterness the narrow social ideals current in their own class, protests against the absurdity of Socialists denouncing the very class from which Socialism has sprung as specially hostile to it. The Fabian Society has no romantic illusions as to the freedom of the proletariat from these same narrow ideals. Like every other Socialist society, it can only educate the people in Socialism by making them conversant with the conclusions of the most enlightened members of all classes" (pp. 6–7).

will. Conversion and the question of revolutionary violence are already linked in *The Devil's Disciple* and *Captain Brassbound*; the association will continue in *Major Barbara, Androcles and the Lion*, and *On the Rocks*.

THE RHETORIC OF THE APOCALYPSE

Twenty years after Shaw's first piece of work for the Fabians, the 1884 *Manifesto*, which became Tract 2, the likelihood of violence and indeed the necessity of being prepared to commit violence came back into his political speeches and writings.* The reasons for this change are not clear, though the divisions over the Boer War and an increasing restlessness and militancy of all groups except the Fabians may have had something to do with it. More likely it was simply a sense, after twenty years, a new century, and middle age, of being farther from the goal than ever.[12] At any rate, from about 1904, Shaw in speaking to socialists would tend increasingly to strike the note of Undershaft's master, who wrote up, "NOTHING IS EVER DONE IN THIS WORLD UNTIL MEN ARE PREPARED TO KILL ONE ANOTHER IF IT IS NOT DONE." In Shaw's political utterances, however, the violence was thrust to the farther end of the revolutionary process, whose proper road remained parliamentary action; and the responsibility for releasing the violence was laid upon the forces of counter-revolution. In October 1904, about the time he was contemplating *Major Barbara*, Shaw declared to his fellow parliamentary socialists, "Parliamentary action is usually the first stage of civil war. ... It is of course possible that Capitalism will go under without a fight; but I confess I should regard any statesman who calculated on that as an extremely sanguine

* Tract 2, written before the Society had repudiated catastrophism, resolved "That we had rather face a Civil War than such another century of suffering as the present one has been." Even so, Shaw had to assure the future general secretary of the organization "that it was all right since in fact no such alternative would ever be offered" (Pease, p. 43).

man."* In his 1908 preface to *Fabian Essays*, Shaw wrote, "The Fabian knows that property does not hesitate to shoot, and that now, as always, the unsuccessful revolutionist may expect calumny, perjury, cruelty, judicial and military massacre without mercy. And the Fabian does not intend to get thus handled if he can help it. If there is to be any shooting, he intends to be at the State end of the gun. And he knows that it will take him a good many years to get there."†

The prospect of apocalyptic revolutionary violence as an answer to inclusive institutionalized disorder becomes explicit in the plays for the first time in *Major Barbara*. *Major Barbara* begins where the Unpleasant Plays left off – with a demonstration of complicity as young Stephen learns the source, in Undershaft's Death and Destruction factory, of the good things he has taken for granted in his mother's house. This motif, slight and comic in the opening, becomes central and tragic in the body of

* Quoted in Bentley, *Bernard Shaw*, p. 11. The passage is from a three-part series in the socialist paper, *The Clarion*, on the myth of "The Class War." One of Shaw's chief points is capitalism's extraordinary success in creating an "irresistible" praetorian guard from the members of other classes whose immediate interests are bound up with those of the capitalists.

† *Essays in Fabian Socialism*, pp. 291–2. At about this time (27 February 1909) Shaw wrote a letter to the organizing secretary of the Fabian Society which shows him more the Fabian than ever with regard to Fitzthunderism. The pertinent passage rejects precisely that strategy Shaw employed in the Unpleasant Plays (short of producing the rabbit of socialism). Shaw wrote: "We must discredit this futile business of beginning with a crushing indictment of the Government and of society at large, and then fizzling out into a perfectly useless platitude to the effect that the only real remedy is Socialism. I think I shall make an adaptation of Comte's law of the three stages, and teach the movement that the revolutionary stage of Socialism in which the patient breaks away from all his moorings, and sets up a vague but fierce revolt against every human institution from his father to the Prime Minister, is the stage in which he is no use even as an agitator, except to the Individualists ... ." (In C. E. M. Joad, ed., *Shaw and Society: An Anthology and a Symposium* (London, Odhams Press, 1953), p. 177–8). It is worth noting that Shaw does not claim that the useless "revolutionary stage" can be altogether omitted from the evolution of the movement or of its individual adherents, nor does he here reflect at all on the likelihood of *ultimate* revolutionary violence.

the play as Barbara suffers Undershaft's demonstration of the grotesque complicity between religion and active charity on the one hand and the profitable manufacture of whisky and weaponry on the other. Barbara, like her audience-surrogate predecessors, is "beggared" – robbed of spiritual assurance and ethical object, of a vocation. But the play does not end with Barbara at this painful point; the dialectic continues, and the unstated third alternative of the earlier plays is now stated.

The end of the play, where Barbara finds her vocation again through Cusins and Undershaft, points directly to revolution not as the piecemeal achievement of a permeated socialist parliament nor even as the last stage of the erosion of private property, but as the only avenue of transformation. It is dominated by Undershaft, who, in his role as Industrial Capitalism, is given his devilish due for creating a private model of state capitalism, organized and welfarized and prosperous enough to be nearly revolution proof. But Undershaft, who has made the best of his chances in the present order, is by no means committed to its permanence or desirability; and he tempts Cusins, now the focus of action, with catastrophist propositions. These are *dramatically* validated in that the new audience-surrogate, poet, classical scholar, and lover, delicate of health and archetypal man of peace, finds he must assent to them in spite of himself. Undershaft proclaims the folly of a world that "won't scrap its old prejudices and its old moralities and its old religions and its old political constitutions" – hardly an evolutionist point of view. He declares that killing is "the only lever strong enough to overturn a social system." "Whatever can blow men up can blow society up. The history of the world is the history of those who had courage enough to embrace this truth." He dares Cusins to "make war on war." This is the challenge that "beats" Cusins, who reveals his desire to arm the common man with "a democratic power strong enough to force the intellectual oligarchy to use its genius for the general good or else perish." Cusins ultimately yields to the temptation of Undershaft – who has shown him the kingdoms of the world – because it appears, in his own questioning phrase, that "the way of life lies through the factory of death." "Yes," Barbara declares; "through the raising of hell to heaven and of man to God, through the unveiling of an eternal light in the Valley of The Shadow."[13]

The words, from Barbara's final rhapsodic aria, recall a final crescendo in Shaw's immediately preceding and exceptionally successful play, *John Bull's Other Island.* Peter Keegan's vision of heaven is of a millennial New Jerusalem, to contrast with the present reality which to Keegan is hell.* The earlier play presents the dichotomy of action (Broadbent) and intellect, including imagination (Doyle), both divorced from spirit (Keegan) or from an informing ethical object. The union of the three in a mighty redeeming trinity is not possible in the anarchic and exploitative society of the play, the present reality; and is only projected, as a madman's dream, in Father Keegan's vision. In *Major Barbara,* however, the whole play moves to the union of the three: of Undershaft, who makes power for the world to use as it will or must; of Cusins, the man of intellect and imagination who can envisage alternative realities and channel the energy accordingly; and of Barbara, the woman of spirit and redemptive purpose, who can rescue both energy and intellect from pointlessness. The end of the play – the residual impression – is pleasant rather than unpleasant, although the union has such a clear parallel with the end of *Widowers' Houses.* The difference is between a depersonalizing ratification of the exploitative relations of the present in which all are bound and implicated and a compact for the future, a union of gifts and qualities rather than of economic interests, which is to transform society. And because one member of this union – the

* "In my dreams [heaven] is a country where the State is the Church and and the Church the people: three in one and one in three. It is a commonwealth in which work is play and play is life: three in one and one in three. It is a temple in which the priest is the worshipper and the worshipper the worshipped: three in one and one in three. It is a godhead in which all life is human and all humanity divine: three in one and one in three. It is, in short, the dream of a madman."

power and efficiency which are the fruits of capitalism – is rendered as the factory of Death, as the power to destroy, there is no room for a hope of evolutionary gradualism in the emotional logic of the play. In its residual impression is the sense that the weapons of destruction must be turned to good ends quickly, or they will continue to ravage mindlessly and pointlessly, out of the sheer momentum of anarchic capitalism. They exist to destroy and coerce, will not cease to exist of themselves, cannot exist without functioning, and therefore must be used to make the revolution.*

Apocalypse – the raising of hell to heaven by high explosives – does come at last in *Heartbreak House*; and thereafter a Day of Wrath, a Day of Judgment, and embodied millennial visions recur time and again, dramatized as a literal rising of the masses (*On the Rocks*), as the descent of a more than literal angel with trumpet from the flies (*The Simpleton of the Unexpected Isles*), as a reported quantum leap to the next orbit (*Geneva*), or a biological leap to a life span of 300 years. Unquestionably it was the First World War that released or demanded such dramatic correlatives; but there were sufficient earlier intimations, as in *Major Barbara, Androcles,* and even *Misalliance* with its successful descent of the gods from the machine.

The emergent image of apocalypse, like that of conversion

* That *Major Barbara* began as an Unpleasant Play is made clear in Sidney P. Albert's revealing article, "'In More Ways Than One': *Major Barbara*'s Debt to Gilbert Murray," *Educ. Theatre J.* xx (May 1968): 123–40. In Murray's own words he and his wife found Act III of Shaw's early draft, "in which the idealists surrender to the armament industries ... a terrible disappointment to us and, I think, unsatisfying to Shaw himself" (p. 124). Murray's written suggestions to Shaw, "to get the real dénouement of the play," made Cusins "come out much stronger, but I think that rather an advantage. Otherwise you get a simple defeat of the Barbara principles by the Undershaft principles, which is neither what one wants, nor so interesting as the ... right way out: viz. that the Barbara principles should, after their first crushing defeat, turn upon the U. principles, and embrace them with a view of destroying or subduing them for the B. P.'s own ends. It is a gamble, and the issue uncertain" (p. 126). As Mr. Albert shows, though the play remained "indisputably Shaw's," these in fact are the lines along which his revision developed.

earlier, requires a glance at one of Shaw's most extraordinary essays, written just as he began the first of his "Plays for Puritans." "The Illusions of Socialism" (1896) divided "the chief means by which Socialism has laid hold of its disciples" into two kinds of illusion: dramatic and religious. The dramatic illusion dealt in capitalist villains and worker heroes; the religious illusion "presents Socialism as consummating itself by a great day of wrath, called 'The Revolution,' in which capitalism, commercialism, competition, and all the lusts of the Exchange, shall be brought to judgment and cast out, leaving the earth free for the kingdom of heaven on earth, all of which is revealed in an infallible book by a great prophet and leader. In this illusion the capitalist is not a stage villain, but the devil; Socialism is not the happy ending of a drama, but heaven; and Karl Marx's 'Das Kapital' is 'the Bible of the working-classes.' "[14]

Also an essential part of the religion of socialism were "salvational regenerations" and edifying conversions; and though Shaw in this essay shows himself suspicious of the most spectacular converts, "the suddenly and fervently impressionable," yet he recognizes that it is the will, shaped by feeling and imagination, that is the motor, not the reason, and that conversion has to precede rationalization. So it is that Shaw's plays, however antipathetic to illusion, however reductive their tactics, however much they depend as comedy and drama on the play of intellect, nevertheless are aimed at altering the condition of the will. It is no accident that conversion became an important idea and event in his plays, or that – despite his dramatic attack on the melodramatic and diabolic view of capitalism – he wrote plays at all. There is such a thing, Shaw declares, as a "necessary illusion" – defined as "the guise in which reality must be presented before it can rouse a man's interest, or hold his attention, or even be consciously apprehended by him at all." (pp. 408–9)

In *Heartbreak House*, however, the intention is not to invoke apocalypse as part of a "necessary illusion," but rather to recognize it, and record it, and proclaim it. The strategy is still salvationist, although salvation is stripped to its barest essential, to the grace that is prior to finding a vocation and a cause. Ellie identifies it as the immanence of "life with a blessing."

The strategy is directed at a new generation, the children of Pease's restless generation of the eighties and nineties. Ellie is the audience-surrogate, the character who learns and the focus of concern, an outsider to Heartbreak House, which is in the hands of the generation of England before the War. On Shaw's part, then – and this helps account for the remarkable, complicated mood of the play – there is something that amounts to a rejection of his own generation. Ellie is to be saved from it and its members, however remarkable their virtues – from their futility, their snobbery, their cultivation of sensibility and the private emotions, from their liberal tolerance of greed and incompetence, from the paralyzing fastidiousness of the humane as well as the wooden insensibility of the capable. But liberation from the generation that had allowed the blind drift to a senseless disaster is not enough. The break with the past is not to achieve a greater anarchy; and so Ellie's new realism, after her disillusioning, is put in communion with Shotover, with the spirit (or reminder) of a remoter, more heroic, demonic, and apocalyptic past.

When Shaw teases his audience about the play coming to an end, Mazzini Dunn, who has outlived his revolutionary heritage, assures everyone that "It wont end ... Life doesnt end: it goes on." Ellie however rejects this view: "Oh, it cant go on for ever ... life must come to a point sometime." Since there is no conventional plot to predetermine an ending in audience expectation, there is no reason for the play not to imitate life in just going on for as long as an audience can stand it, or in coming unexpectedly to a point.

It comes to a point, of course, to our relief, in an apocalypse; but the moment itself is complicated. On the one hand the bombing – as Captain Shotover twice declares – is the judgment. It is the war, come as a judgment to the generation before the flood; for the play begins when Shaw says he began the writing, in the atmosphere of the years before. There is, terribly enough, a great joy and release in the danger and destruction, a joy which had its analogy in the war fever, and is the other face of the weariness, boredom, and heartbreak of the interminable grinding muddle "in which nothing ever does happen." The audience is implicated in this terrible joy, both through its pleasure in the spectacle of courage and in its natural desire for an ending.

On the other hand, the judgment, this ending, may be a beginning. Life does come to a point; but *also* life goes on. The characters allegorize the events in a hopeful way, though the allegory is much overweighed by the literal truth of their joy in destruction. There is revolutionary optimism in the purging of Boss Mangan and Billy Dunn "the two burglars ... the two practical men of business" who lose their lives in trying to save them, and in the fact that "the poor clergyman will have to get a new house." The recollection of Proudhon's "property is theft" in the equation of the burglar and the capitalist (the two thieves of contemporary civilization between whom the heart is crucified)* reinforces the hope of what can come when destruction has cleared the ground. But the final joy is, unhappily, at the prospect of further release in destruction.

The prime source of apocalyptic expectation in the gospels is directly relevant to Shaw's secular apocalypse. In *Heartbreak House* as in the gospels, the Judgment is only the last act of a drama of salvation. The salvation motif pervades the play: in Captain Shotover's transactions with the Devil in Zanzibar, in Ellie's account of the poverty that damns by inches and money as a means to salvation, in Shotover's Calvinist reckoning of the saved and the damned, the two degrees of humanity and "the enmity between our seed and their seed"; in the Burglar's dodge

* In documenting "The Illusions of Socialism," Shaw observed that "Labour is commonly described by them as crucified between two thieves, a fancy picture which implies, not only the villainy of the landlord and capitalist, but the martyred sinlessness of the Socialist ..." (p. 408).

for extortion by claiming a call to salvation; in Mangan's canvas of who besides himself is going to "save the country"; and of course in Ellie's quest for "life with a blessing." The Judgment itself recalls the accounts in both *Matthew* and *Luke*. (Shaw later uses the former as the explicit basis of the action in *The Simpleton*.) Matthew incorporates an allusion to Noah (and, it would seem, to the world of *Getting Married*, *Misalliance*, and *Heartbreak House* before the war):

> For as in the days that were before the flood they were eating and drinking, marrying and giving in marriage, until the day that Noe entered into the ark,
>
> And knew not until the flood came, and took them all away; so shall also the coming of the Son of man be.
>
> Then shall two be in the field; the one shall be taken, and the other left.
>
> Two women shall be grinding at the mill; the one shall be taken, and the other left.
>
> Watch therefore; for ye know not what hour your Lord doth come.
>
> But know this, that if the goodman of the house had known in what watch the thief would come, he would have watched, and would not have suffered his house to be broken up.
>
> (*Matthew* 24: 38–43)

The house in the play – appearing to the audience at first in the guise of "*an old-fashioned high-pooped ship*" – is also an ark of Society, a "soul's ship" and a ship of state threatened by the rocks. The two in the field, the two women, the goodman of the house and the thief, those taken and those left, all have their echoes in the play.

Luke follows the Flood comparison with a further reminder of Lot and Sodom, where "they did eat, they drank, they bought, they sold" until "it rained fire and brimstone from heaven, and destroyed them all." It continues with some advice on reactionary impulses respecting the *status quo ante* (advice Hector seems to make a point of following during the airship attack):

> In that day, he which shall be upon the housetop, and his stuff in the house, let him not come down to take it away ...
> Remember Lot's wife.
> Whosoever shall seek to save his life shall lose it; and whosoever shall lose his life shall preserve it. (*Luke* 17: 28–33)

The advice on conduct in those last days is literally borne out in the instructive fates of those who try to hide in the gravel pit as opposed to those who present themselves to the thunder. But the idea of the saving loss is also embodied in what Ellie earlier experiences as "heartbreak."

Heartbreak House is by no means the end of Shaw's anti-Fabianism in the drama, but it is the point of full emergence of what is most essentially antithetical to Fabianism: apocalyptic catastrophism; not as a warning to the enlightened and unenlightened to take another route, but as an acknowledgment of the failure of the enlightened and of the alternative route.

Fabianism of course had been changing too, especially under the impact of the war, which led even the Webbs into designing an at least partly revolutionary Constitution for the Socialist Commonwealth of Great Britain (1920). The practical program of the Society, however, became all the more democratic and parliamentary with the permeation and formal conversion of the Labour Party to socialism; while Shaw, even in his straightforward political writings and speeches, grew more and more savage over the hopelessness of parliamentary democracy. Webb's famous "inevitability of gradualism" Shaw maintained as an inexorable fact, vindicated by Soviet Russia's return from instant collectivism to Lenin's New Economic Policy. But political and economic catastrophism were no longer identical in Shaw's thinking, and gradualism was much discredited in his eyes as a means of achieving control, of effecting a revolutionary transfer of political power. In 1888 Shaw spoke of "a gradual transition to Social Democracy" through "the gradual extension of the franchise; and the transfer of rent and interest to the State, not in one lump sum, but by instalments."[15] In 1928, in the chapter on Revolutions in his *Intelligent Woman's Guide to Socialism,* he still argues that the transfer of political power *need* not be bloody, but on the analogy of the nullification of Irish Home Rule and the French and Russian experience, he makes the peaceful acceptance of the parliamentary way to socialism seem exceedingly unlikely. His pessimism is acute here; for while the necessity for transformation remains absolute, the probable violence to come he sees as dead loss, as the destruction of the necessary capital and industrial base for socialism. By 1932, however, this dilemma has been resolved by economic collapse and the enormous dissipation of resources and accumulated capital even in the absence of revolution; so that Shaw can speak "In Praise of Guy Fawkes" on a Fabian platform because: "Guy Fawkes wanted the Government to do something, and saw that the first thing to enable the Government to do anything was to blow up Parliament. I think it is very much to be regretted on the whole that he failed, because ... the whole history of Parliament has been a triumphant vindication of his grasp of the situation." In that same lecture he declares, "I do not want the catastrophe to be deferred. I am impatient for the catastrophe. I should be jolly glad if the catastrophe occurred tomorrow. But being an average coward ... I would rather that the catastrophe were settled without violence."[16]

From *Heartbreak House* on, Shaw's plays embody an ambivalence in feeling about revolutionary violence and coercion which is not, however, an ambivalence in expectation. Nor is there now a discrepancy between Shaw's plays and his politics. The earlier discrepancy, which I have been trying to understand and put in some perspective, grew out of a conviction, based on Shaw's private experience, about the roots of action; and out of a perception of a "contradiction" in the Fabian program itself. This perception appears in the 1896 essay on "The Illusions of Socialism." The dramatic and religious illusions of socialism are necessary to enlist and energize the will; yet they have it in them to destroy or at least nullify the socialism they instill – to prevent the realization of socialism. The superiority of socialist illusion to the "flattering" sorts that merely sustain the *status quo* lies, says Shaw, in its contact with fact and "its power of bringing happiness and heaven from dreamland ... down into living, breathing reach." Yet "when the reality at last comes to the men who have been nursed on dramatizations of it, they do not recognize it. Its prosaic aspect revolts them." They are offended by its coming in "penurious installments, each maimed in the inevitable compromise with powerful hostile interests ... Hence they either pass it by contemptuously or join the forces of reaction by opposing it vehemently." Alternatively they became impossibilists.*

Illusion – which is necessary – automatically generates disillusion. The "contradiction" was not soluble, but to be lived with apparently, and dealt with by applying Jevonian questions as to the degree of utility; that is, by regulating the creation of religious and dramatic enthusiasm to secure an optimum utility. This Fabian strategy, however, is simpler than that of Shaw's plays, which instead of seeking a judicious mean, put the extremes in tension. The plays use a double strategy: on the one hand of disillusion, urging the *acceptance* of reality and the attractions of a clear-seeing realism in the course of exploding various "flattering" illusions; on the other hand, of conversion, revolutionizing the will by conducting it to a *rejection* of reality – that is, of the present pernicious impasse. The necessity of living with contradiction and holding in tension fact and desire was central in Shaw's brand of Fabianism and is apparent in his dramatic method. Consequently, in his earlier plays, the idea of a transforming apocalypse could exist only as an emotion to which the logic of a rejection of the present reality led. It could exist in his plays as a real event when apocalypse – the religious

* *Selected Non-Dramatic Writings*, p. 417. There are traces of Comte in Shaw's essay; but it is noteworthy that Shaw makes the positive stage of socialism – socialism as political science – a third stage of illusion, albeit more useful and more refined than socialism as religion and socialism as allegorical drama.

illusion – had entered reality and become the common experience.

NOTES

1 "Sixty Years of Fabianism: A Postscript by Bernard Shaw," *Fabian Essays*, Jubilee Edition (London, 1948), pp. 207–8.
2 Edward R. Pease, *The History of the Fabian Society*, 2nd ed. (London, 1925), pp. 17–18.
3 *Fabian Essays*, p. 29.
4 *The Fabian Society: What It Has Done and How It Has Done It*, Tract 41 (London, 1892); reprinted in *Essays in Fabian Socialism*, Standard Edition of the Works of Bernard Shaw (London, 1932), pp. 126–7.
5 *Essays in Fabian Socialism*, pp. 60–1.
6 *To-Day. Monthly Magazine of Scientific Socialism*, x, n.s. (August 1888): 35–9.
7 *Ibid.* (September 1888): 78–80.
8 *Ibid.*, p. 41.
9 *Widowers' Houses*, Independent Theatre Edition (London, 1893), p. 117.
10 *Ibid.*, p. xix.
11 See, for example, "The Illusions of Socialism," in *Selected Non-Dramatic Writings of Bernard Shaw*, ed. Dan H. Laurence (Boston, 1965), p. 418.
12 See the suggestions of A. M. McBriar, *Fabian Socialism*, pp. 82–3.
13 Quotations are from the 1908 Constable edition, *John Bull's Other Island and Major Barbara*. Later editions show significant variation.
14 *Selected Non-Dramatic Writings*, pp. 415–17.
15 "The Transition to Social Democracy," *Essays in Fabian Socialism*, p. 43.
16 *Platform and Pulpit*, pp. 241, 257–8.

Index of Plays